Dedicated to my Family

My Husband, Stuart,

My Kids, Sami and Danny

& my Step kids,

Chrissy, Stuart, Jessi, and Joey

And my Black Lab, Bo,

Who never brings me the stick!

Thank you all for my incredible happiness!

A Mother's Memories

Rhonda Rayl

Chapter One

I love that I have such a short drive home from our office. I rarely even get to listen to a whole song on the radio before I am pulling up my driveway. Sometimes I even take a little longer route just to enjoy listening to a song that I like, especially one that reminds me of driving around with my kids as they were growing up. If no one is looking or driving by me on the road I am always singing and dancing like full-crazy-young-girl mode! Makes me feel so good to bust out in song! It seems that most of the music I hear gives me a memory of something that happened in my life. And that is usually a good feeling since most of my life has been full of awesome memories that I want to relive over and over. Life just goes so fast. It seems like I was just a kid, then next I was just married, next thing you know I was having my own kids, and now I am dealing with each one growing up and going off with their own plans for life. What happened to all that time? All that life I always wanted and dreamed about? All I ever wanted for as far back as I can remember was to be a wife and mom. I remember everything like it just recently happened, yet it was so long ago and now all of those things are behind me. I want life to slow down because I don't want any more of it to be over with quickly.

    I sat a little longer than normal at the last stop sign before I turned onto my street just taking in all the beauty around me. Our house is the last one before the intersection, but because we have so much property, after making the turn I still have a ways to go before reaching our driveway. On our side of the street are tall pine trees lining the road until you come to our yard which is lined with a long white split rail fence that ends at the beginning of our driveway. The right side of the drive is bordered with a wall of huge rocks we found in our woods. We used our backhoe to bring them from the woods and place them there. We planted hostas all across the top that grow and spread all over the tops of the rocks in the summer covering them in sweet shades of green and tall sprouts of lavender flowers. The other side of the drive is lined with large Red Maples, our favorite type of tree.

    Across the street from our property there is a beautiful golf course. The entire green is concealed behind all different kinds of trees and bushes. We can see the course only after all the leaves have fallen in autumn. By then there are no longer golfers out so all we see is the beautiful, green, grassy fairways and all else is silent. The exception to this silence comes on Friday and Saturday evenings when the banquet center continues to host events like weddings just as they do throughout the entire year. If we are in our front yard, we can hear the music and people laughing from the beautiful old dairy farm with its huge silos which has been a golf course and banquet center since 1968. I always tell Derek, my husband, we should become wedding crashers and go enjoy the fun!

    Throughout the golfing season, although you can't see anyone on the course with the obstruction of the trees, you can hear the soft "pop" in the distance whenever someone drives the ball. It actually is all quite peaceful. On hot summer afternoons I like to lie on my float in our pool and open up a good book. I usually don't get far before my eyes are closed, however, tranquilized as I hear the golf balls being tapped and cars as they "whir" by soothing me into a dream. At that moment, a really loud car or motorcycle screams by my house at full speed and wakes me, sometimes almost making me flip off my float into the water!

When I am alone I do a lot of thinking. Sometimes I think about our business, from planning meetings for possible new clients, to creating designs and scheduling jobs for our current ones. Other times I am thinking about my kids, my husband and housework. I hate housework. My favorite thing to think about is the fond memories I have had throughout my life. Every memory I have has made me what I have become in my life.

Back during my own childhood, I remember the times I spent with my sister and my parents just sitting at home every Friday night for game night. Sometimes, my sister and I each would have two to three friends show up because we would tell them all how much fun we had. It really was something we enjoyed and looked forward to doing so all our friends came to us since they knew they couldn't get us to do anything else on a Friday night! They all enjoyed spending time with my mom and dad as much as we did. My parents were always there for my sister and me, always supporting us no matter what it was we wanted to do. Even if it involved getting up at 4am on a Sunday morning to drive us to my best friend Beth's volleyball competition three hours away. We didn't even play on the team, we just wanted to be there to support our friend. They would take us and cheer her on to a victory right by our sides! I wanted to be that kind of parent when I had kids too!

But the best memory of my childhood was meeting and marrying my true soul mate, who also had a great childhood, and then we were blessed with four healthy children. We were sure to plan as many family activities as possible so our kids had the same great experiences we did. All the things we have done from watching our babies learn to talk, walk, and grow, to camping and birthday parties, where each kid always insisted on a white cake with sprinkles! And then, of course, carrying on my family tradition of the

Friday game nights. I even added a tradition of my own to our game night. We start by cooking and trying a new recipe together every week. It is so fun being in the kitchen with my husband and kids talking about how our week has gone, and it has taught all my kids to be good cooks as well!

But today it was hard to concentrate and it also wasn't a *happy burst into song day*, because my own happy thoughts and memories were overpowered by the talk show hosts on the radio. I usually don't even pay attention to them. When they start talking I just change the station to find another song, but today their voices were somber and it made me turn up the volume to focus on what they were saying as I cruised up my road.

They were talking about a local girl that had gone missing quite close to where we live. How scary. They didn't know if she was abducted or a runaway, but were leaning more toward the abduction due to evidence found where she was last seen. She had been missing for almost two days now. She is only fifteen years old and is homeschooled, so I am not sure if any of my kids would know her. I will have to ask them. Sad world we live in sometimes that these things happen, I hope she turns up alright.

I pulled my car onto our new concrete driveway that we just had poured last week. My mood had gone from fabulous to completely heartsick in a matter of three minutes. All I could do was think about how that could have been one of my own children and I couldn't even fathom how her parents must be feeling right now. I tried to make myself think of other things so I didn't walk into the house so completely dismal looking. My son wouldn't like to see me like that if he was home.

"How about this driveway?" I forced a good thought, "It sure is nice and smooth" I continued to say out loud to myself. Derek just took off the yellow caution tape last night so I knew I could drive on it for the first time today.

Up until now, if we wanted our windows to be open along that side of the house, every car that drove in caused a cloud of dust from our old rock drive to billow in and settle all over our furniture. I couldn't keep it clean even if I dusted every day, but I also didn't want to keep the windows closed because I loved the fresh air flowing through the house. Now that issue was solved with this new driveway and, extra perk, our cars were staying cleaner also.

I happened to glance up at the oil change sticker in the upper left corner of my windshield and it was due for maintenance. I guess I could drive the new truck while mine goes to Evan's garage. Derek kept our old truck as a work vehicle so we wouldn't beat up on the new one. I pushed the garage door opener on my visor and turned into the garage my husband had just finished building for us last year. Derek is very handy. He has done construction his whole life so he has learned to do everything from painting to building and he has taught himself to fix most anything. He just hates working on cars. His brother decided construction wasn't for him anymore and he loved working on cars so he opened his own garage. So now he and Derek barter their specialties to each other.

Our home is over a century and a half old. It has been in Derek's family since it was built in 1859. Derek rented it from his grandparent's right after he graduated college. The large house had gotten too big for them to take care of in their old age and they wanted something smaller. They really wanted to keep it in the family and Derek was actually the only one in his family that wanted it since he knew he could do all the repairs himself.

They worked out a deal where he

would rent for a couple years until he was at a job long enough that a bank would trust him with a loan. The house had not been updated in at least thirty years when he first got it. While he was renting he ripped off old wallpaper, replaced all the worn carpeting, and installed all new windows, a water heater, a furnace, and a roof! We started dating that same summer he got the house so I really got into the idea of helping fix up such a great old house. I painted all the walls in the house while he stayed just ahead of me doing the ceilings. It was so fun because he let me pick all my favorite colors for all the rooms inside.

Together we chose the paint for the outside. Tan with wide white trim around the new windows and ditched the old shutters. We finished it with a beautiful auburn front door and added a full glass storm door to show it off. What a difference some paint makes!

Next, we did all the floors. We picked out carpet for the bedrooms, living room and family room, a wood looking laminate in the dining room, and some tile in the kitchen and bathrooms. We continued to work on the house together every day after work. After a full year had passed by us we couldn't believe how much better the house looked. I hated leaving every night to go to my parent's house because not only did I hate leaving Derek who I had fallen helplessly and hopelessly in love with, but I also felt the same way about this wonderful house that we were making a home. We made the decision to get engaged and move in together that second summer together and used both of our incomes to get the loan to pay his grandparents for the house.

    We had put so much money and love into it we didn't want to take any chances of it not being truly ours. Happily our parents gave us their blessing knowing neither one of us wanted to get married just yet, although we knew that would for sure be in our near future.

    I suddenly realized I was just sitting in my car in the garage thinking about how much fun those first few years were when Derek and I were alone. Of course adding the kids only enhanced our love for each other and completed our dreams of having our family, but thinking ahead, it seems that Derek and I will be just a twosome again in the near future. I know we will be fine but I still am going to miss having all the kids here. Especially since we just did even more renovations and made the house even bigger than it was all those years ago.

The house had plenty of rooms and a decent amount of square feet, but it was cut up a lot and there was no way to join two rooms together to make one large family room. When our families came for holidays we were always spread out throughout the house and couldn't really all be together in one room. This usually worked out okay since the girls would take the living room, the boys headed to watch a game in the family room, and some of us stayed in the dining room and kitchen to talk or play cards. We realized there wasn't going to be one room big enough for even just our own family to be together on something incredibly important like Christmas once they were all married and had families of their own. So for the past two years, in his spare time and weekends, Derek has made our home more of our dream home by extending our family room into a very large great room with cathedral ceilings and big windows overlooking our pool and land.

He also then attached a two story, five car, heated garage. Upstairs of the garage is our new master bedroom suite with a master bath and huge walk in closets. Then the other side has a separate workout room that we all can enjoy. If that's what you call working out, *enjoyable.* It is now perfect for whatever we decide to have here.

Next thing we need to do is we will work on getting moved over to the new bedroom within this coming week or two hopefully. Then our oldest daughter, Kayla, who has the only bedroom on the first floor of the house, will move up to our old bedroom, and we will turn her bedroom into a first floor office. It will be nice not to have the desk and filing cabinets in our upstairs bedroom and make working from home so much easier.

Although we felt a little like we were kicking Kayla out of the only room she's ever known, I really needed the extra space when I have to work at home. Now if I want to work early in the mornings or late evenings I won't bother Derek anymore if he is sleeping in our room. I debated about making the extra room off our new bedroom above the garage the office instead of a workout room, but our family always makes pros and cons lists when we make decisions and everyone decided all these arrangements worked best for everyone.

Another small drawback for Kayla is that our other daughter, Olivia, will share the old master with her. She will be leaving for college in less than a week so she won't be home often enough to really be in Kayla's way. Especially with the size of the room. It has its own full bathroom that includes double sinks and a long counter for them to share and the room also has two separate closets so they will have plenty of space. This frees up Olivia's old room so one of the boys can move over to it since they have shared a room since Johnny was born. They haven't decided which one of them is going to move over yet, we are letting them decide. Both rooms are the same but one is on the front of the house and one is on the back. They both are telling the other it doesn't matter to them if they move or stay so if they don't decide soon we may have to help them figure it out. Even though the girls are older we felt it was only fair to make them share since they have both always had their own rooms, and won't be home as often since they will be busy with school. Plus it was time for the boys to get their own rooms before they graduate and possibly move out.

    Kayla is twenty and is still at home while she is working her way through airline stewardess school and working at the airport. When she is done, she would like to be a stewardess on international flights so she can see the world and she won't be home very often. Therefore, we decided she should stay with us instead of wasting money on an apartment right now. The boys are starting ninth and eleventh grade this year so at least they get to have their independence in their own rooms for a few years before they go off to college or the military, whatever they decide. Oh wow, there I go again, daydreaming. I can't believe I am still just sitting in my car in the garage!

    I got out of the car and grabbed a diet coke out of the garage fridge that is always stocked with pop, beer, water bottles, and some snacks for Derek for when he works outside. Because of our house being so big, at one point a family member made it into two separate living spaces and had a renter in one side. When Derek's grandparents bought it from that cousin they turned it back into a single family home.

    Derek's Grandma wanted her kitchen to face the sunrise so Grandpa left the kitchen on the far side of the house and turned the other kitchen, which is on the driveway side into a laundry room and mudroom where they would come in and kick off their shoes. Therefore it's kinda backwards because the kitchen isn't off of the garage like most homes would be. When we added on we debated about moving it to the new addition to make an open concept kitchen and family room instead of one large family room and then making the old kitchen a sunroom. But I really like how big the new addition was going to make our existing family room and didn't want to break it up into a kitchen and family room so we left the kitchen where it was.

    Besides, while we were deciding on how to make the addition work for us, I told Derek that as we get older I want to hang out together in a family room, not the kitchen. If the kitchen is part of that area I will always be in it, cleaning and cooking. My fear was after the kids are all gone I will be so sad that all I will probably do is eat! Therefore it is definitely better to keep the kitchen far away from me! So we just stuck an extra fridge in the garage so whoever was outside didn't have to come through the whole house just to grab a drink. I smiled at these thoughts to myself as I walked in the door.

    As soon as I did, I was immediately greeted by my big, old, black lab Bo, who was always awaiting my arrival even if I am only gone for ten minutes. They often show videos of how excited dogs get when their owners return from overseas from military tours of eight months to year. They have nothing on me and my Bo.

"Okay, Okay. Calm down, we're gonna go as soon as I change my clothes and get my tennis shoes on!" I calmly, yet sternly told him while I pushed him to keep him down and tried not to laugh. I sat on the bench by the door and removed my shoes.

Bo continued to jump up and down, whined and whimpered and ran in circles with excitement as though I was gone an entire week! He still acts just like he did when he was a puppy. It was like telling a kid we were going to Disneyworld! Any mention of the word "walk" and his ears would perk up and then all the commotion would begin. Today it was different, I didn't even say the word, all it took was for me to walk through the door. I guess because we do walk almost every day as soon as I get home he is expecting this routine. Up till now, when I would come home he would just stare at me, anticipating the first words out of my mouth, which were always, "Hey Bo, do you want to go for a walk in the woods?" He loves to run on the trails that we made in the woods that covered our property all around our house.

My husband and sons actually made the trails years ago so they could ride our four wheelers all throughout our property but they also worked great for walking the dog, or should I say for "running" the dog? I got up and walked through the house to the kitchen to see if Johnny was home. He was my youngest son, and our only non-driver so you couldn't tell if he was home by looking for a car like you could for everyone else. As I entered the kitchen, Johnny was there eating his lunch.

"All he does is see me anymore and he goes nuts." I said about the dog.

"Mom, why don't you wait until you've changed and are actually ready to go so he isn't jumping all over like that?" He asked while scarfing down his sandwich.

"I know, I didn't even say anything this time." I said laughing. "Anyway I think it's so cute how he knows what we're gonna do and how excited he gets."

Johnny just shook his head and continued to eat his chips. I can't believe how fast and how much food that boy can put in and never show any of it anywhere on his body. Both my boys are very athletic. They love working out and playing sports, especially football. Johnny is fourteen and this will be his first year playing football for the high school football team so he won't be doing the two a day practices his brother does, only evenings. He also helps train the youth football in our small town at a football camp that goes in the mornings. Everyone that meets him, especially little kids, look up to him and admire him. He has a kind heart and is always joking around making anyone that is around him laugh all the time. My older son Dakota is sixteen and just got his license, he has already started his practices earlier this summer with a weeklong football camp in a canoeing town about two hours away. It's the longest I have ever been away from one of my kids and I hated it, so I know I won't do well when Olivia leaves.

    I headed on upstairs to change my clothes with Bo trailing so close behind me I swear I could feel his breath on my ankles. When I turned and glanced behind me his tail was still moving about a million wags a minute. It was like he was smiling with all his teeth showing and his tongue hanging out!

    As I reach the top stair I look over my soon-to-be old bedroom. Although I can't wait to move into the new addition, I love this room and all the memories we have had in here. From the intimate times with Derek to our kids not feeling well and having to climb into bed with us for a night or two. Sometimes we did sleepovers when they were little especially if there was a loud storm that kept them from wanting to be in their own rooms. They would all bring blankets and pillows and gather together on our floor. We would have popcorn and watch movies till they all dozed off peacefully. If the power went out, we would huddle on the floor with them with flashlights and make up stories about how the thunder was the angels bowling and the lightening was created when they got a strike!

Our house has two sets of stairs. One goes directly to our bedroom and the other set leads up to a hallway to the kid's rooms. Our room takes up half of the entire second floor. Still, as I admire it I realize I have neglected it. There are clothes in a basket that need put away, dust that needs wiped off the dressers, and a vacuum would feed for a day on the lint and animal hair all over the carpet.

At one time Derek wanted to change our room to hardwood flooring. He says that's what a lot of his clients have been doing. Not me, nope, I love my bare feet on the carpet. Right now it has a Berber type carpet; I would love a shaggy one, so that's what I am getting in the new master bedroom. Kayla and Olivia actually love the carpet in this room because it's a beautiful creamy tan that will go with anything they decide to put in here.

As I think of this I only get a crooked half grin because I wouldn't care if my kids all lived at home with us forever. I really don't want them to grow up. Time just goes so fast, I swear just yesterday they were learning to crawl and feed themselves, now it seems like they don't really need me for anything, but to put a roof over their head.

That's just fine by me though, any need that keeps them close to me I will take. I found some comfy shorts and a tank top to change into then grabbed some socks out of the drawer and my tennis shoes off of the treadmill which I also can't wait to have out of my bedroom!

Don't get me wrong, I love the treadmill. Every day when I wake up I get on for thirty minutes to an hour to get my blood flowing for the day. It's almost as good as a cup of coffee to get the day going. But I still have lots more of that once I go down to the kitchen, just because I love coffee! Derek's idea to make a workout room on top of the garage was a great idea. Now we can also fit a weight bench, an elliptical and a flat screen television so any of us can work out whenever we want without everyone actually coming into our room to do it.

As I sat on the edge of the bed and tied up my old worn out walking shoes, I realize I need to make the time to get to the store and get some new ones. The treads are almost completely worn down on these and if I walk fast in the woods I slip too easily on the leaves and loose dirt. Bo wouldn't even let me tie up the laces. He was pushing up against me and rubbing me with his wet nose trying to move me along.

"Come on, give me a minute to tie my shoes!" I chuckled.

And then I started thinking how much I have been enjoying the summer. I think a lot. Especially with the kids not needing me as much, I am always either thinking of a project I can do, a new recipe to try, and start to mentally see my grocery lists for what I will need to make them, or I help Derek with design ideas for work. I am always thinking about how different we can remodel someone's existing place to make it the most usable for their family, and I think about my kids, mostly about them. But right now I am thinking about how beautiful it has been outside. My very favorite season of the whole year is summer. I love being in shorts, a t-shirt, a ponytail and a pair of flip flops, or a good ole' pair of broken in tennis shoes when I go on my walks, of course these particular tennis shoes seem so beyond that.

The summer is a time to retreat to the beach and build sand castles with the kids and walk out to the lighthouse on the long break wall and especially to go camping. Both Derek and I grew up camping, it was the first thing we found we had in common. We started tent camping when we started dating and slowly upgraded every couple years and now we have a nice thirty-one foot travel trailer with opposing slide outs in the front living room area that gives plenty of room for all of us to spread out.

Although I am very happy with this one being my final purchase, Derek would like to upgrade one more time to a fifth wheel cause I guess they are supposed to be easier to pull for longer trips.

Owning our own business, and having some good, trustworthy employees and independent contractors, it was always pretty easy to take the time as the kids grew up to do a lot of fun things. We have always had season passes to an amusement park about thirty minutes away from our home. I could take the kids while Derek was at work since I can do a lot of my work for him from home. We actually bought my SUV that seated nine so I could fit some of the kids' friends to make it even more fun when we went there. A few years back they closed that amusement park which was very sad for our family because we shared so many good times there.

    I guess it doesn't matter anyway cause the kids were getting to the age of sports and jobs and their own driver's licenses so we had stopped going anyway. My whole family enjoys the sunshine, however, who doesn't really? We love hosting and going to cook outs, taking camping trips to see new places, and not having to worry about a bunch of homework! Best of all, the water at the lake warmed up so nice this year.

    Most of the camping trips we take each summer are either right on Lake Erie or on one of the smaller lakes within three hours of home. Since we spend a lot of time in the water, it sure makes a difference if the temperature is more comfortable. We have a couple of jet skis we picked up from one of Derek's clients. They ran into some financial issues and couldn't finish paying for some work Derek had done for them. Derek saw the jet skis sitting on their trailer and asked if he wanted to pay with them and the trailer and call it even. The guy was more than willing to settle his debt that way instead of owing us the money. They have been great for us to play with on the lakes we camp by that allow them, but we are thinking of upsizing to a boat that we can all fit on and pull a tube or water ski behind it so we can all play at the same time. If we do decide on that I have to pull it behind my vehicle or leave it somewhere. Right now I don't know if I am capable of pulling more than the jet skis. I keep wanting Derek to show me how to pull the camper just in case he ever gets sick while we are out and I need to get us home, but when he agrees to teach me I always chicken out! I laugh at myself while I think about this. Derek says "The bigger the trailer the easier it is to back up." But I am still a chicken! I am just too afraid to try.

    See my problem is, due to always thinking a lot, I often jump from one thought to another so quick I lose people. My mind is always going. But I think my worst trait is always being worried about things, including the fear of people and things getting hurt or messed up, so I try to avoid situations that could cause that to happen. My kids get mad cause if I hear an ambulance or a fire truck I call them on their cell phones to see where they are and make sure they are okay. I tell them to just deal with me cause I am a mother who cares therefore I worry.

See now, what was I thinking about, oh ya, back on track. We also like camping along rivers so we can spend our days canoeing, tubing, or kayaking downriver and just enjoy the whole day on the water. We have two kayaks, a canoe, and plenty of river tubes in case the kids ever want to bring friends along for a trip. Now, the river water is always pretty chilly compared to the lake water, but it's so fun once your body kind of gets a little numb, you don't even notice.

We had a really great summer this year. I was sure to cram in as many camping trips and days to the beach as possible with whoever was available to go. It just wasn't the same with the kids being older and not all of them being able to come every time due to sports and work schedules. I am really trying to convince myself that them getting older is a good thing cause Derek and I will be alone again someday like we were in the beginning of our marriage. We will be able to do all the things we used to be able to do like our other friends with grown kids are enjoying now. But then immediately I think of how I am so busy cooking, cleaning up after the kids, and planning our days that I just will be so bored when it's only the two of us.

    This takes me to thinking about that missing girl again. I forgot to ask Johnny if he knew her. I can't even imagine what her mother must be going though. They live close to us, maybe I should send a meal. I am sure if my child was missing, the last thing I would want to do is cook, let alone eat. I could also mention this to my church friends to help. I wonder if she belongs to a church. I need to look into all of this later after we walk.

Chapter 2

I just realized that the kids' summer break is pretty much over. It seems to fly by anymore. Back when Derek and I went to school we didn't start classes until after Labor Day weekend. Now in our area the kids go back at the end of August. I guess it's okay though, because then they get out earlier in June when the weather is getting so nice they don't want to sit through classes anymore. They can't wait to start hanging out by our pool as often as they can, and I love having everyone here! But when they do go back it's weird not having a bunch of kids by the pool all day long, hanging out and enjoying the sun, laughing together, and just being kids. It seems once Dakota starts his two-a-days football practice and Johnny has his football practice in the evenings at the beginning of August, things start to calm down a little bit around here. Then just a few weeks after practice starts school and homework begin, and then the pool is hardly ever used.

We usually avoid putting the winter cover on it until we are tired of vacuuming out the leaves that are falling off of the trees every day. Next thing you know it's time to close it down and cover it up until the following Memorial Day weekend comes around.

We only have three good months to swim here in northeast Ohio, usually around Memorial Day through Labor Day. And the worst part about that timeline is everything we like to do is in the summer, swimming, boating, fishing, camping, cook-outs, just being outside in the warm air. We cram it all in and it makes the summer fly by.

We usually camp every other weekend starting in late May to early September so there is about seven weekends we don't even use the pool at all, but there is always someone in it during the week and the weekends that we are home. When we aren't home we have extended family that love to come over and enjoy it. We like the idea that our house is rarely without people around it so it is never left empty. I love just the ambiance of sitting around the pool and I really love that so many others get to enjoy it too. Now with the new addition on the back of the house having such large windows I can sit with my morning coffee or evening dessert and enjoy it even longer. As for right now however, we still have what's left of summer and we still have some beautiful days ahead of us.

    Bo started to nudge me with his nose and rub his body against my knees even more. I hadn't realized I had been just sitting on the edge of the bed daydreaming all this time while he was waiting so patiently. See what I said about thinking quietly about everything and anything all the time? People always tell me to snap out of it, and I realize I went there again. I am just so happy with my life, I love to replay it in my head often. I smiled and kind of laughed a little out loud at my own thoughts as I stood up and headed back down the stairs, again with Bo on my trail. If I told everyone about my life they probably wouldn't enjoy my story as much as I have enjoyed living it, so this is my own personnel way to have my own fun.

"See ya later Johnny. You need me to be back to take you to football or is Devon's mom picking you up?"

"Ya, I do need a ride, Devon's family went out of town for one more week at their cottage before school starts."

"Wow," I replied, "You mean he is willing to miss football practice?"

"No, his parents made him go. His mom said that one day he would be all grown up and she wouldn't be able to make them spend family time together so as long as he was under her roof he was going…or something stupid like that."

"Oh, I see what she means, I hope all of you still want to go on vacations with us when you get older, I sure would miss you."

"Mom, we will always go with you. We are all going to buy campers and line them up along a river for a week every year so our kids can do all the things we did growing up. We all talked about it, no matter where we live we will meet down in Mohican Valley every year."

"Awww!" I said trying not to cry. "I am so glad you all love it that much!"

"Yeah, we all have bets on which one of us will have the biggest camper." He said smiling. I'm gonna get a big 36 foot fifth wheel and pull it with a 350 Ford diesel pickup truck!"

"Wow I bet Dad would love to have that also!" I said with a grin. "Ok, I'll be back in time to run you up to the school. Let's go, Buddy." I said quickly as I grabbed my cell phone and we ran out the door.

I never leave without my phone. I always want to make sure my kids or husband can find me no matter where I go. I don't like leaving notes, I would be afraid they wouldn't see them. They can always call my phone. I even have a special ringtone song for each member of my family, even my mom, which I had programmed into my phone so I know who's calling.

Olivia set my phone up that way; I'm not that knowledgeable about new technology, she seems to be the brightest one of our bunch when it comes to that stuff. Actually, when it comes to anything. I just don't know where her brains came from, but I am happy she got them from somewhere.

However, common sense is another story, she doesn't have much of that. The rest of us are loaded with it, which I guess is just as good if not better than having the book smarts a lot of other people have. Hopefully the boys will be able do all that technical stuff when she leaves for school because my husband and Kayla stink with technology also.

    I started thinking even more. I do most of my thinking during my walks because it's so quiet. What Johnny said really made my day! That would be the best vacation ever. Just imagine all of my kids and their families with our campers for a week every summer. I can just imagine all my grandkids running around. But that's real far away I hope. Right now I hate to even think of my kids growing up and moving out of our house to go to college or anything that makes them not a child anymore. I need to get my mind on something else.

    What was I thinking of before I talked to Johnny. Oh yeah, the different seasons. The other two seasons I like are spring and fall. Spring is nice because the snow all melts away and the green leaves begin to grow back on the trees. Then we start seeing more of the beautiful blue sky as the winter clouds disappear. All the pretty flowers and other perennials soon start to pop up out of the ground and add radiant color around everyone's yards. I wish that tulips and daffodils lasted all summer long, they are so cheery and colorful and you don't have to keep them watered like all the annuals I add around our pool every year. I've joked a few times that I was gonna add plastic flowers to the flower beds so I didn't have to keep them watered, but I would never be able to do that. I really enjoy how big and full my flowers get over the summer and all the wonderful comments I get from everyone about how beautiful my yard looks. Derek and I went to some classes and found out which flowers bloom throughout summer so as some die off others bloom.

    The other season I enjoy is fall. Fall is a beautiful time of year because the trees decorate the sky as their leaves turn warm shades of red, orange and yellow. I love going for drives and seeing all the different foliage across the hill sides. The colors just seem to cascade all over them. It's just so amazing how all the different colors come originally from a green leaf but then can become so vibrant and beautiful!

    The best part of this season is watching my boys play football. I just love hearing their names announced over the speakers each time they make a good play. Then all the parents around me high five me like I did something! I just say,

"I just birthed him, he does everything else!"

As everyone cheers and laughs. Johnny is really good at faking that he has the ball. All the tacklers from the other team jump all over him while the quarterback runs off with the ball and sometimes makes it all the way for a touchdown before their opponents see he doesn't have it! I learn more every year. I was never a fan of football until they started to play. The ringtones Olivia gave me for the boys are these crazy "pump up" football songs that I never heard before. I think I will have to think of songs I would like to attach to my thoughts of them cause those are horrible!

I had them in baseball when they were younger because I knew the game. Then they told me they really didn't like baseball and really wanted to play football. I was so bummed cause I hated football. It just seemed to be boring and go on forever when I saw it on tv. Then Derek started to explain how the game worked and I started really enjoying it. I am still not sure of all the positions of the players and what they do, but I am slowly getting it.

I hate when football season ends though because that means the fourth season, my least favorite, is right around the corner.

I wish I could live where I only saw my favorite three seasons, because the fourth one I could definitely do without. The one season where everything seems too cold, almost all the time. Good ole winter. It's a pain in the butt to go anywhere without shoveling mounds of snow and ice off of sidewalks and driveways and brushing off your car, and by then you are so cold, wet, and tired you don't want to go anywhere anyway. At least that's my perspective.

Before the new garage, my car and Derek's 1966 mustang were the only two that fit in the old one, so I was the only one that didn't have to always brush off the snow, but if Derek was using the garage to work on some things at home for a job, like cutting trim or building a cabinet, then I would get kicked out cause the mustang has never seen the snow. Now Derek and I both have a spot for our main cars, a spot for his treasured mustang, and a spot for his work truck, and he still has room for a work space for him in the fifth bay.

He put five doors on one side for us to pull our cars in and then on the opposite side facing the pool there are three more doors.

When we have our parties we will take out our cars and set up tables and chairs from our church and open all the doors and it will be like our very own pavilion! Kayla says she loves the idea so much she will have her wedding at our house someday with the beautiful back yard and my cooking. Little does she know I would have to have that catered!

    I giggled to myself. We also have a two car, two story barn that was built thirty years before the house in 1829. We keep the mower, four wheelers, and jet skis out there, and upstairs of that Derek made the kids a game room with a pool table, foosball, and some video games. This is their favorite place to hang out with friends, especially when the pool is closed for the season.

    Derek even made parking spaces between the garage and the barn complete with parking meters we picked up at a flea market for the kids cars or any friends that come over. Everyone thinks it's a pretty cool idea, even though we don't make them put the money in them to park there. I laugh to myself.

    See how I get off track so easily? Back to my winter issues. As I get older, the one thing I have noticed that is a good thing about winter is I get a lot of things done in my house. It is always clean, very organized, and

I also get caught up on a lot of movies and television programs. That's because the other three seasons I am never inside unless I am working on our family business or doing chores that have to be done like cooking and laundry. I am either camping, working in the yard, playing in the pool with my kids, going to the zoo, amusement parks, the beach, anything I can do to be outside.

One time I went in the closet to get something and looked down at my vacuum. I thought,

"Wow, when was the last time I used that?" I chuckled at myself and thought, *"I hope it rains soon so I can clean this house!"*

Who wishes that? Probably only someone like me, who refuses to stay in the house with only limited beautiful outdoor weather each year. They have a saying in the Cleveland area.

"If you don't like the weather, just wait a minute and it will change!"

But Bo doesn't care what the weather is like, all he cares about is when I come through that door and I mention going for a walk. Our long walks in the woods are the highlight to his day! And I really enjoy an easy way of sneaking in some extra exercise into my day.

"Oh Bo, what a beautiful day it is!"

The bright blue sky had just a few white puffs of clouds resembling cotton softly floating above us. I think those are called *Cumulus clouds,* stupid names these scientists give things that don't even resemble the item they are describing, I would call them *Cotton ball Clouds*, then everyone would know exactly what they were as they floated by! I would love to be able to float up and just cuddle up in one, they look so soft.

The wind was still and the sun was beaming. I turned my face up towards its warmth and closed my eyes just to feel the rays caress my face. Then I looked back down and opened my eyes and took a glance around me. Our yard is so beautiful with all the perennials and the big, round pool. Derek built a deck all the way around it, so when we have company over, everyone can fit around the deck to watch their younger kids swim, or the older kids can all hang out together. Then there's the times in the evening when Derek and I just sit together with the pool lights on and have some iced tea. Long Island ice tea, actually. I smile to myself, maybe there's a possibility of that tonight if Derek doesn't get caught up at work too late. We would like to add a gazebo with a hot tub on one side, but

Derek's been so busy with the business he hasn't had the time to even design it! Maybe I could figure it out, although I have never designed one before.

We keep two acres of our land mowed as neat as a golf course and then there is almost eighty acres of woods behind us that are great for walking and four wheeling from the beginning of spring till the end of fall. Derek and our boys ride out with four wheelers and drag out old dead trees that have fallen and chop them up to use in the wood burner in that dreadful season that I hate so much.

As we finally begin our walk, Bo runs as fast as he can to get to the paths in the woods, and boy is he fast. He runs all the way to the opening in the trees to enter the path, then back to me, then back to the opening again. It's as if he is saying, "Will you hurry up already?" And I have to admit, I was being very pokey, just enjoying everything Derek and I have accomplished together. Today for some reason I was really being thankful for my life. I am not sure why today I feel different than any other day. This is pretty much my schedule of events almost every day of the week so it's funny that I am feeling so strongly today about really observing it all so closely. I think it may have something to do with my Olivia leaving.

When we get to the opening to the woods, he runs down the path so far and so fast you would think you would never see him again. But then just as sudden as he runs away, he runs back at full force, just to make sure that I am following him. Then, off he goes again. He does this the entire time that we walk. He doesn't always stay on the path either, once we get in kind of deep, he runs all over the place. He hops, runs, and sniffs, every time like it is always new to him. It is so entertaining to watch him have so much fun. And I like these excursions because it's another kind of exercise I do enjoy besides my treadmill, so we both win. I would love to take him every day, but I am very involved with my four kids and all their activities, and our business.

I am the one that writes all the quotes and takes care of all the accounting and bookkeeping. I sometimes get to help the clients chose colors, when they ask for my input, and I am also pretty good at helping with the drawings for the different jobs.

Everyone says I should have been an interior decorator or an architect, but I love my life I have with Derek. I wouldn't change a thing. With all I am involved in sometimes it's too hard to get out here every single day. But we do take about a twenty to sixty minute walk back here at least four to five times a week.

I should be taking Bo to more populated places more often so he can get used to walking on the leash and seeing all the people. Bo really loves people, almost too much. He barks, whines and tugs on his leash continuously as all the hair stands up on his back and it looks like he wants to attack. Then when he gets up to them he loves them to death.

The leash is another story. I really have to get him more comfortable with it. He is so used to not needing one at our house and in our woods that he drags you and bites at it when I walk him anywhere else. I just hate keeping him on it when he seems so much happier running free. I know it's all my own fault for not having him trained by this time in his life.

Oh well, it is what it is, so it just works out best to only walk him in our own woods. But still if I don't take the time to try to get him used to it soon, I'll have to hire a real trainer. It would just be nice to be able to take him to more places. Especially camping.

He stays at my parent's house when we go away because he would just bark and whine the entire trip. Also we are away from our campsites a lot hiking, shopping, sightseeing, or in the boats so he couldn't do all that with us and would be confined to the camper just tearing the place up as people walked by it and he is unable to get to them.

Along my walk I see the trail markers Derek made for me. My husband is wonderful. He will do everything and anything to make my life easier. A couple years ago, in the late fall when the leaves had fallen across the path, I lost my way and had to call Derek to tell him I got lost in our own woods. He told me to listen and follow the sound of cars to get me to the road nearby. I thought I would follow the sun but it was high in the sky because it was so close to noon I didn't know which way it was going. I actually ended up about a mile up our road by the time I came out. I don't know how I got off track so badly. When I get out here it's so peaceful, I start thinking of everything I need to do at home and work.

And then of course that darn daydreaming that I do. But it just makes me happy. When the path is clear it's easy to stay on no matter what I am doing because it's very easy to see. However, when the leaves fall or it snows you really need to pay attention where you are going. After that one time that I let my mind get the best of me, Derek decided to mark all the trees along the trail with a large dot of blue spray paint so if I lose the trail in the autumn or the winter, I can just follow the marked trees and I won't get lost again.

Sometimes it's very comforting to look up and see the blue dots, even when I don't need them, just because it makes me think of him and how lucky I am to have someone that cares about me that much in my life forever and always. He really is the perfect man for me. I smile whenever I think about him and all the wonderful things he has brought into my life, especially our children.

"Bo!" I shouted, "What are you sniffing now? We have to keep moving." Sometimes he sniffs a little too long, and I would like to keep the momentum up so I can get a little bit of a workout. But I can just walk right by him because he always catches up quickly and flies right past me anyway, then of course comes running back again. He just loves this!

Today I noticed there sure seemed to be a lot more trees down than I have noticed on my other walks. Derek would be excited to hear about that. He loves coming out to get them. I think it's his way of "playing" with our boys. He works a lot during the week because his work is so admired everyone wants him to work on their house, but I told him weekends are for family time, so he never works on the weekends. Sometimes he gets so busy he doesn't get home during the week until the kids are ready for bed.

I know it's his working so hard is how we have all of the nice things that we have, and how we are able to take a lot of weekend camping trips. He always reminds me that if he works hard now and we stash our money away, we will be able to retire early, and move to the south for the winters. So there are no complaints here. I would love to get away from the snow all winter and then come back from spring until fall. I love watching the change of three of the seasons.

Looking around I can see that some of the leaves have already started to change color. They sure are radiant when they first change. Soon all the leaves will fall and cover the ground as if mother nature is changing the flooring on her house. Then they all get brown and crunchy and it's fun to walk through them and make a lot of noise!

I looked farther ahead, deep into the woods. One of our neighbors has a sugarhouse on the outer edge of our property. We let them tap our trees when the sap starts to flow around the beginning of March, and they give us free maple syrup all year. Derek always makes Belgium waffles every Sunday for him and the kids, they all love that stuff. I, however, think the thick waffles are like eating cake for breakfast and real maple syrup is too sweet for me. I actually like the store brand light or sugar free stuff, if any, and a blueberry or strawberry toaster waffle because they aren't so thick. I don't want to hurt Derek's feelings though so on Sundays I have eggs or cereal, and then I enjoy my crispy waffles during the week after he has gone to work. The neighbors have invited us over to watch how the syrup is made, we haven't made it yet. I will put that on our list for things to do.

I usually make a list for each season of fun things I want to do with my family and we hang it on the fridge and have fun marking things off as we do them throughout the year. Like in the summer it's always camping, but it might say to try a new campground, or it may say to see a waterfall, walk to a lighthouse, and go see fireworks, catch a jar full of lightning bugs, or build a sand castle and have a picnic at the beach.

In the fall, some ideas would be to go to a pumpkin patch to pick out a pumpkin, go to the Fall Fest that our hometown throws on the old fashioned square up town, find colored leaves and make a collage, build a scarecrow, or have some warm apple cider.

Then in the spring we can plant new flowers, go to a festival, or go to a drag strip, and possibly take in a museum we haven't seen.

Finally in the winter, we could go ice skating, roller skating, the movies or go bowling, and my favorite for this year, I want to build a snowman laying down on a beach towel in my front yard with a beach umbrella over him and some flip flops and a cool drink with a little umbrella in it! Maybe we will make a sign that says "Is it summer yet?" How fun is that?

Usually in winter, because I just can't stand getting cold, Derek takes the kids outside and hangs out with them doing all the wintery stuff while I stay inside and bake cookies or bread and nice warm casseroles or stews, and then I am always sure to have a nice pot of homemade hot chocolate waiting for them all when they come back inside.

As we walked, if that's what you want to call it cause Bo continued to run back and forth, I realized how quiet it was for the first time. I'm sure it's always this quiet, I just never noticed it before. Lately I have been becoming more aware of the little things that happen around me. With Olivia leaving home to go to college in North Carolina this coming Friday my heart is heavy. This will be the first child to move away.

My family is extremely close. I think that's why Kayla decided to stay home while she goes to stewardess school, although I can't believe she is going to leave us to travel the world. I will believe it when it happens. I want my kids to do well, and succeed, that's how Derek and I raised them, I just never thought how much it would hurt if they had to move away. Olivia and Johnny are super close also and have the same humorous personalities. If it were up to them, he'd go with her to school. I just don't know what our family life will be like without her around.

"Well we are almost done, Bo," I said. "Did you have a good time?"

Isn't it funny how people talk to their animals like they would actually answer back? I swear my animals, I also have a cat, want to tell me stuff. I just can't figure it out all the time. My cat is more vocal than my dog. She will cry loud if the water bowl is empty, and if she is outside she meows so loud you could almost hear her across the entire house to let her in. She follows you around, even to the bathroom, and just meows and meows. I would love to know what the heck she is trying to tell me.

"Okay, we're done, was that fun? I just don't understand why you don't just come out here once a day and do the path yourself, Bo, you know it well enough." I said laughing.

The short trail that we did today only takes about thirty minutes to walk. Bo could run it in a quarter of that time if I could keep up.

"Now what?" Bo was acting like he wasn't done playing. "Oh. I know, okay go get a stick." He loves this game. He will find a stick if you tell him to, but the only problem is he will drop it within two feet of you and when you try to get it to throw for him to fetch he grabs it first and runs with it. Another reason to hire a good trainer.

"Bo, give it to me," I demanded. Nope, just as I leaned for it off he went. "Okay, I'm not playing with you then." I said as I walked back toward the house.

Chapter 3

I headed back through the yard, with Bo trailing close behind me. I needed to take Johnny to his football practice. I went into the house to get a drink of water and take my asthma medicine. I hate taking any kind of medicine, except vitamins, if those count as medicine. I still don't want to believe I actually have any ailments that have to keep me on any kind of medication for any long periods of time. I skip it once in a while, but then I kind of feel a little wheezy after a few days, especially if it's been hot and humid like today, so then I take some. It seems like if I take one pill every three or four days, instead of everyday like I am supposed to I can keep my symptoms under control, but then I feel like the asthma and the medicine aren't controlling me! Probably not a good idea, but I have the fear that twenty years down the road they will blame my organs shutting down on all the stupid medicine they always had me on so in my head this is better.

"Come on Johnny, let's get going" I yelled up the stairs.

"I'll be there in a minute, Mom," he replied.

No one else was home yet, they should be soon. I was contemplating what I should make for dinner. Maybe chicken. I pulled out some chicken breasts and through them on a plate on the counter, if they don't thaw in time for dinner maybe I will just bake them frozen with some Italian dressing, they'll thaw while they're cooking. Johnny appeared and we headed outside and jumped in our new truck, and pulled down the driveway. We just bought a brand new Ford F250 pickup truck with an extended cab, and I know Johnny likes riding in it so that's why we took it instead of my SUV. It's really sharp. My husband wanted one so badly, he says it will tow our camper better, but our older truck, now his work truck, towed it just fine. He just wanted a bigger "man car". It all just makes me laugh. I always try to teach the kids that material things aren't what matters and I know they understand that for the most part, but it is hard when Derek likes to enjoy spending the money he works so hard to make for us. Johnny was unusually quiet on the drive to the practice. As we pulled into the parking lot he asked,

"So, how was your walk?"

"Great, you should come with us, it's nice work out."

"I get enough of a workout here, Mom, maybe you should stay here with me and try what I do every day!"

"I'll have to pass; I wouldn't want to show you up in front of all your friends." I said with a chuckle. "Hey, by the way, did you hear about the missing girl in town? I guess she is home schooled now."

"Yeah, I heard about it when I was over Jackie's. She said they played together in elementary school before she started homeschooling and then they just grew apart. It's really sad, hope she's okay. Picking me up at 6:30 right?" He asked.

"Yep, see ya then, love you Honey." Jackie is Johnny's girlfriend.

"I love you too, Mom, forever and always."

He always tells me he loves me and it feels so good. Some kids grow out of that, but not mine they all still tell me every day. I sure have some warm hearted kids. They have always wanted to spend time with Derek and me. And they have always been helpful around the house and have really never given us any trouble as of yet.

I hear so many stories about problems with kids, especially teenagers, and I just feel so lucky to have all of mine just the way they are. We often say "forever and always" to each other after saying I love you. It is something Derek and started before the kids came into our lives and we just continued it with them and they seem to like it. Currently a country singer made a song with a very similar title. It is called "Forever and *For* Always" and it is perfect for Derek and me. It's as if she knew us and wrote it for us. I made it my ringtone on my phone for when he calls me.

On my way home, I pulled through McDonald's for an ice cream cone. So much for my walk. Derek calls this "justification". I do a little exercise so then I can have the extra calories to spend. This explains why I never lose any weight when I work out because I always "justify" it with more treats. Exercise seems to make me even more hungry anyway. Oh well, I'm happy, and I am not that out of shape. I'm the same weight I was in high school and I have had four kids, so I would say I'm doing just fine. My girlfriends say it's gonna catch up to me someday, but I have always exercised, drank a lot of water, and ate pretty healthy for the most part so I'm not worried.

When I return home my three older kids were all there by the pool. A sight I like to see. It's nice that my kids like to hang out together. I was actually surprised to see there wasn't a ton of other kids with them. We usually have a pretty full house. I'm happy that everyone enjoys themselves here. I feel like having everyone here all the time is what has kept me so close to my own kids. Kayla is sunbathing, she is tall like her Dad, with the same dark hair but my blue eyes. She also has the longest thickest, eyelashes I've ever seen. You would think she glues them on daily.

Olivia is the complete opposite of Kayla with looks and personality. She has my blond hair and Dad's dark brown eyes. She better have layered on the sunscreen or she will fry like chicken! She is eighteen and just graduated high school with honors and a full ride on academic scholarships to the University of North Carolina in Chapel Hill. When she leaves in three days I won't get to see her again until Christmas break! I keep thinking how hard this is going to be for me because we have always spent a lot of time together.

Actually, it would be very hard if any of my kids moved far away. Of course I do want them to succeed on their own, and move to their own homes, and eventually have families. I am just so afraid that jobs may take them far away from home and we won't be able to visit as often and still have dinners together with them and their families. I want all the kids to be here for holidays, summer cook outs, and especially camping. I always tell them they have to marry someone that enjoys camping, and they have to buy campers so we can at least go on one or two family trips a year together. That's why I was so happy when Johnny confirmed they all felt the same way.

Dakota jumped into the pool with a big splash! Everyone always thinks he is Olivia's twin. They are just about the same height, Olivia is a little shorter, and have all the same features. He made the varsity football team last year right before starting his sophomore year of high school. He's always been a lot like his dad, a real hard worker. His practice is called "two-a days" because they practice from 8am-3:30pm with only an hour break for lunch, if that's what you want to call it, because all through lunch they study plays on paper.

Johnny has light brown hair and brown eyes. We aren't sure where the light brown hair came from, we always thought it would eventually get blonder since it wasn't as dark as Derek's and Kayla's, but it stayed light brown. We had all our kids two years apart, and when it was time for one more addition, we got the cat, and then two years later we got Bo. That made our family complete.

"Hey guys! Did everyone have a good day?" I asked as I walked up on the deck of the pool.

"Oh, Mom," answered Kayla. "Today was so fun. We learned how to use the emergency exits on the plane, and we got to jump out onto these huge blown up slides!"

"You jumped on a blow up toy all day while I sweated my butt at practice?" Dakota joked.

"I didn't say it was easy." She answered slyly; she got up off of the lounge chair and made dramatic motions with her hands, legs, and face as she told about her training.

"First, we had to warn all of our practice passengers of the imminent danger and we gave them instructions of what they had to do. Then we had to bust open the emergency exit door, and once the slide inflated, Jenna and I had to be the first ones down. It was so big, like an enormous air mattress, we jumped out the door, hit the mattress with our backs, bounced a little and slid to the bottom. As the other attendants helped the passengers onto the slide we had to catch them at the bottom, and we had to move fast. There were little kids, who were easy, but there was this really big lady, and Jenna and I just looked at each other and realized we had better catch that one together!" She laughed and went on with more excitement.

"Of course to make things even more difficult, they had the fire department from the airport spraying us with their hoses like we were in a storm. So we had to try to be very serious, but it was actually really funny!"

"Sounds like playtime, not work or school." Dakota said as he dived into the pool again.

"How was your day, Olivia?" I asked.

"Well, I said my good byes to everyone at work and they bought me a going away cake and gave me a card filled with money to help me get some essentials when I get to school. It was harder than I thought having to leave everyone, but they were all excited for me to be going to college and my boss told me to let him know when I am home on break and he will be sure to give me some hours. On top of that he already talked to the owner of another sub shop in the same franchise within walking distance of the dorms, and as soon as I get settled in at school he said to come see him about working out a schedule for me around my classes. So that will be nice and I can have some extra money for things my scholarship doesn't cover." She sounded so excited.

"Just don't work so much that you ruin your scholarship. You have to keep your grades up or you will lose it." I replied.

"I know Mom, I will just work a few hours on the weekends to pay for odds and ends and have some spending money. I already told him that weekdays are for school and studying. By the way, where were you?" She asked.

"I dropped of Johnny for his football practice. I can't believe he is starting the high school. You guys are all growing up so fast! I'll have to pick him back up later. But for now I think I'll go get my suit on and join you all out here until I have to start dinner and go back for Johnny."

"Sounds great, Mom, hurry back there isn't much sun left!" Kayla yelled as I headed for the house.

I went inside, and found my suit. I really should pick up another swimsuit for this year. I like to wear a different one in lakes and rivers than the one I wear in clean pools. I had three up till last year but two were all worn out so I tossed them. Maybe I'll go to the mall this weekend after Olivia is gone so I have something to do to keep my mind off things. I went back outside and joined my kids back at the pool.

"Hey, Mom?" Olivia chimed up.

"Hey, what?" I answered.

"I can pick up Johnny for you because I am going to go rent a movie to take over Sara's house later and Kayla is going in to make dinner so you can relax the rest of the night."

"That would be great. Practice ends at 6:30, he needs to be picked up before 7pm or the coaches get really mad." I said.

The girls are always so helpful with their brothers. I am lucky to have kids that all love each other so much. I got out my float and laid it in the water and then gently laid across it. It felt so good to cool off in the water after a long hot day.

"Kayla, I have some chicken breasts thawing on the counter, do whatever you want with them."

"That's perfect." She replied. "I have some stuff I picked up also I want to try, do we have Italian dressing?"

"Yeah, in the fridge, that was my idea too." I told her about my plan if the breasts were still frozen.

"What else did you get, Kay?" Dakota asked.

"It's a surprise!" She said smiling.
"Oh great." Dakota seemed nervous.

He had reason to be. Kayla liked to experiment in the kitchen. Sometimes it was something great, sometimes we have had to order pizza. I just smiled and laid my head back on my float, I didn't care if she made peanut butter and jelly, all I knew was I wasn't cooking dinner tonight.

Chapter 4

Derek got home pretty late and missed the awesome dinner that Kayla made for all of us. Usually if he is stuck at a job his clients will feed him dinner, which is pretty nice of them. We don't usually worry about him, we just pack leftovers for his lunch the next day.

Derek was lucky enough to land a great job painting this mansion about fifteen miles from home, but he needs to get it done before the fall weather starts to get too cold for the paint to dry. They like his work so much they already have him lined up to do a lot of inside work over the winter and have passed his name on to their friends, who are also looking to have some remodeling done. This should keep him and the guys busy for a while. He is hoping to hire about two more employees so hopefully soon there will be enough of them that they will just work a regular work day and be home by dinner every night. He really clicks with everyone he meets. People just enjoy his company, especially me. If he gets home too late he usually just says good night to the kids then comes upstairs to our room to shower then we lay in bed and watch tv and talk about our days until we fall asleep.

"Did you have a productive day?" I asked him.

"Yeah, I was able to get a lot done on my list, so that always makes for a good day." He replied. "Did you get those invoices done for the Cunningham project?"

"Oh yeah, and I needed you to look over that bid for the bathroom remodel on the Smith's house. It seems like you aren't including everything you normally do."

"Well, there's a story with that one. Mr. Smith's younger brother from West Virginia moved in with him because he had fallen on some hard times back at home. I guess he does do some remodeling himself, so he's doing the tear out, then I will install all the drywall, tile and do all the fixtures, then I guess he will do the grout on the tiles, sand the mud on the drywall and paint the walls, so it was a weird bid."

"That explains it." I laughed. "I looked at your notes and was thinking to myself you must have gotten tired and not finished before you gave them to me."

"Well, I guess he wants him to earn his keep until he finds work up here. He asked if I could give him a job but I don't need anyone just yet. I told him I would check into it for him with some other people I know. I'll wait until I see how he does finishing the bathroom before I make any recommendations or take him on myself. Oh, Abby, you should see him, I think he has less teeth then Mr. Smith, it must run in the family! Oh yeah, and they asked if they could hunt out on our property, I told him no, but directed him to some places I knew they could go."

"Yeah, that's for the best since we like to be back there a lot, I would hate for there to be people hunting back there. Hey, did you remember to say goodnight to all the kids before you came up?"

"All except Olivia, where is she at?" He asked.

"She is sleeping over Sara's one last time before she leaves for school. Are you still able to get away from work Friday to go the airport with us?"

"I wouldn't miss that for anything. I still think we should have drove her down to college in the new truck and made a vacation out of it." He smiled.

"You know that's not what she wanted, and I have all her things packed and ready to be mailed so they get there when she does. That's what her roommates are doing and she doesn't want to be different. Besides, we already have all of our time off planned when we pick her up for winter break and head for Florida. That will be more fun for the other kids anyway instead of staying at a college campus."

"I don't know, I hear a college campus would be a good time." He smirked and winked my way.

"Stop now you are scaring me. Is our little girl going to be okay so far away from home?"

"Oh, Abby she will be fine. She has always made the right choices. I don't think college will change that."

"I know, she's a great girl, I can't wait for that trip. I love camping honey, but a week in Florida at Disney and then a beach house right on the ocean? You may not be able to bring me back here to all the snow that will be coming." I leaned over and wrapped my arms around him.

"Did you get our entire itinerary worked out for the trip?" He asked.

"Yeah, I think so. Triple A sent us maps, the tickets for everything we are doing while we are there, and they sent more pictures of the hotel at Disney and the beach house. I have all the addresses though so we can just put them into the GPS and follow that."

"I don't always trust that thing. Remember when we were looking for that new campground and it put us in between two cornfields?" He smiled.

"That was so funny, good thing someone answered the phone at that place even though it was off season and told us it was three more miles up the road or we would have had to rough it." We both laughed.

"I also noticed my oil sticker on my car is due, do you have time to do that soon or should I drop it at Evan's Garage?"

"I am pretty busy and Evan owes me a favor, so I will drop it off tomorrow and have him run me back here to get my work truck and you can drive the new truck till it's done.

We might as well drive it more than just to pull a camper since I haven't had much time off to enjoy crusin around in it." He said smiling.

"Okay, sounds great to me, Thanks."

"Hey, I hate to ask but what was for dinner? The house smelled really kinda fishy."

"Kayla made chicken and clams, sweet potatoes and sweet corn. Her friends at work want to have a clambake and so she wanted to see if she liked them first before she paid the $18 for the clambake and then didn't like them." I said trying not to laugh too hard.

"Well, we did teach her not to waste money." We both smiled and lay down in bed.

"Um, Derek?"

"Yes, Honey?"

"She packed the leftovers in your lunch."

He gave me weird look then put his head on the pillow, then we fell asleep in each other's arms.

Chapter 5

Friday came too fast. We all took the day off to see Olivia off at the airport. Dakota even missed his football practice. I woke up early as usual, and rolled over to kiss Derek good morning, but he was already gone. Normally if he didn't have to work he slept in a few hours after me so I went looking for him.

The house didn't smell fishy anymore it was much better. Actually, as I descended the staircase there was a marvelous smell streaming out of the kitchen. I wondered why the girls were also already awake and what they were cooking that was making my mouth water. As I turned to the kitchen I heard deep voices. It wasn't the girls after all, it was the boys. I peeked quietly around the doorway to see what they were up to.

"Make sure you flip those before the chocolate chips burn." Johnny was saying to Dakota.

"I know I've watched Mom enough to know what I'm doing, you just make sure those cookies come out just before their done so they are soft just the way Olivia likes them."

"Okay boys, you're both doing well, where does Mom keep the real maple syrup? Derek asked them.

"The real stuff would be in the fridge, Dad. I think Mom warms it in the microwave in that small pitcher." Dakota told him.

I couldn't believe it. They were making chocolate chip pancakes and chocolate chip cookies for Olivia. They were both her favorites. She could eat the chocolate chips right from the bag. Sometimes when I went to bake cookies there weren't even enough left to make a half batch!

"Don't forget the whipped topping guys." I said as I walked in.

"Hey, Mom, how we doin?" Johnny asked.

"It all looks and smells great, she will be so excited." I walked to each of my favorite men and gave them a kiss on the cheek and thanked them for what they were doing. The girls came into the kitchen next.

"This smells great!" said Kayla. "You didn't have to go through all this work for little ole me. She laughed and nudged Johnny as she grabbed a plate.

"Whatever, Kay, this breakfast is all about Olivia, all her favorites." Dakota responded to her sarcasm.

"This awesome breakfast is for all of us," Dad started. "This will be our last breakfast together until Olivia's winter break, are we missing anything anyone else would like?"

"How about I scramble some eggs real quick so we have some protein to keep us full all morning?" I added.

"Oh no, mom, we got this," Johnny said as he got pot holders on his hands and opened the bottom half of my double oven. "We even made your breakfast egg casserole that you always make for Easter and Christmas!"

"Oh my gosh, you guys are the best brothers ever!" Olivia said as she walked in and hugged her brothers at the same time.

"And you, sir, are the greatest Dad in the whole world!" She moved to her Dad and reached her arms up around his neck and hugged him tight.

"Okay, everyone grab a plate, and line up like a buffet, all this work made me hungry!" Johnny said with excitement.

"You're always hungry, Johnny." Dakota laughed.

We all filled our plates with the incredible food and sat down in our breakfast nook to have one last meal together for a long time. I was trying very hard not to break down and cry.

"Wow! This is the best!" Olivia said as she ate the food made special for her.

"I baked chocolate chip cookies for you to share with your new roommates; you'll make friends fast with those!" Johnny was so proud of himself.

"I love all you guys so much, I just can't believe you all got up so early and did all this for me. And where did you find chocolate chips? I thought I ate them all!"

"We'd do it again, Baby." Derek told her. "It was the boys' idea. They snuck in and woke me up really early this morning to go to the 24 hour Wal Mart and buy all this stuff so we could all this."

"Yeah, it wasn't too hard, good thing your favorite breakfast isn't eggs benedict or something like that!" Dakota added.

After we all enjoyed the delicious breakfast the boys had made, Kayla started to clear the dishes and load the dishwasher.

"Olivia, we have something else for you also. Hang on a minute." Kayla ran to her bedroom and came back just as quickly, and handed Olivia a small box. Olivia smiled at her, and then gently opened the lid.

"Oh my God, it's beautiful" Olivia began to cry. "This is the best gift ever!" Olivia took a chunky bracelet from the box. It was a charm bracelet.

"I don't get it." said Johnny. "I mean I guess it's pretty, but why are you crying?"

"It's a family charm bracelet, silly, for her to have us with her all the time. See there is an airplane, that's me, the hammer is Dad, the two footballs represent the boys, the dog and cat are self-explanatory, the book is you, Olivia, since you love school, and the heart is Mom because she has so much love for all of us."

The girls in our family all cried, as always, the boys just thought it was a cool idea and finished cleaning the kitchen.

"I love this, and I will only take it off for showers. Thank you so much Kayla, I love all of you, forever and always!"

After the kitchen was clean, the boys quietly gathered Olivia's bags that she was taking with her and went out to the truck. We all finished getting ready and then all of us, except Kayla, climbed into the truck. Kayla drove herself because she had to stay and work after Olivia left. The ride started quiet, and then Johnny said,

"So, did you choose to go to UNC to avoid the snow?"

And we all laughed because we all hate the snow. He is always good at breaking the ice and making people laugh.

"I think the whole family should move to North Carolina with me." She giggled.

"I bet when Kayla becomes a flight attendant she will only request to fly to the warmest places!" I added.

"And when I play professional football, it will be in Florida." Dakota smiled.

We all laughed together like it was any other day and then talked the entire way downtown.

Derek pulled into the airport parking lot with Kayla still following along. We all got out of our vehicles and headed inside. We checked Olivia in, which didn't take as long as I had hoped. I was willing to wait in line for an hour just to be with her longer. We decided we could sit in the coffee shop together until she had to go to her gate.

"Anyone want anything?" Derek asked. Everyone shook their heads no.

"You know what honey?" I said slamming my hand down on the counter. "I'll have a strawberry/banana smoothie." I was hoping to break the sullen mood everyone was in.

"That sounds good, I'll have one too." Olivia seemed to understand what I was trying to do and followed with a slap of the hand on the counter and a forced smile.

Then everyone ordered one. We drank our smoothies while Kayla gave us a tour of the airport.

"This place is bigger than I thought." I exclaimed looking all around and up toward the ceiling. Derek and I hadn't flown anywhere since the new airport had been built many years ago.

"Where's your *classroom?*" Johnny asked with a smirk.

"Actually down this way, I'll take you there."

"You really do sit in a class?" Dakota asked amazed.

"We meet in class each morning and go over things like fire safety, customer relations, CPR and even self-defense and some other stuff, and then we go to different parts of the airport to learn all the other things we need to know." Kayla said as she continued to show us around until Olivia had to go to her gate.

We went with her as far as they would let us. We weren't allowed to go any farther because of security so we all said our good-bye's there.

"Well. Olivia, keep those grades up, and be back to your dorm early, and don't forget to stay away from boys!" Johnny said in a deep voice pretending to be a stern father.

He jokes when he gets nervous and I am sure this is starting to hit him as her leaving gets closer. After giving her a long, big bear hug he turned away and I actually saw a tear in his eye. I was going to give him a hug, but I thought I should just let him be.

"Okay, girl, be sure to text me every day, and I if I have any flights your way I will be sure to call you!" Kayla choked up as she tried to be strong.

Olivia dropped her head and I thought she was gonna fall apart.

"I'm not getting mushy, geez, we will see you in December, and do you know where we're all going?" Dakota asked as he put one finger under her chin and tilted up her downed head.

"We're going to Disneyworld!" We all yelled in unison.

Derek and I hugged our little girl separate then together. We told her how much we loved her like a billion times over then Derek gave her one last kiss on the forehead and said, "Remember we love you Olivia, forever and always."

"Forever and always to all of you!" She cried.

And with that she turned and walked toward the gate. She took a few more steps then turned around and waved and blew a kiss. Johnny jumped up like he caught it in the air and stuck it on his cheek.

"That one was all mine, Sis. Now get going before you miss your plane!"

"Ok, I need to get to work so I will see you all at dinner." Kayla hugged us also, spun around and walked swiftly away, probably to pull herself together before class began.

No one talked on our way back to the truck or on the way home. This was weird for us because my family likes to talk, especially

Johnny. But we are also very close and this was the first time one of us was going to be away from home. I wanted to say something to make everyone feel better, but even I was at a loss for words. It was going to be so strange without Olivia being around the house. Every day she would greet everyone with her big bright smile and pleasurable conversation.

As we drove all I could do was think about how fast time had flown this summer and I really wanted it to drag on so Olivia's time to leave never came. The reality was setting in on how old my kids were really getting. My babies were all growing up and soon would all be on their own and away from Derek and me. I had always been so involved and busy with them, I just didn't know what I would do when they all left home for good. I needed time to slow down before they were all gone and I would not see them every day.

We returned home and everyone jumped into their everyday routine. Derek went to the garage to get the mower out so he could do the lawn, and since Dakota had already missed his football practice, he went to the shed and got the weed wacker to help him. I glanced at my watch and noticed I still had a few hours before Johnny started football practice.

"Johnny, you don't have practice for a while, you wanna go in the pool before it starts?

"Actually if you could take me to the school now, the girls are practicing for their powder puff football game, and I would like to go help them out." He said smiling.

"Oh, I see, you wanna *help* them," I winked at him. "Ok. Let's go."

"Cool, I'll grab my bag." He replied as he ran to the house.

Once I got Johnny alone in the truck, I decided to talk to him about his sister leaving.

"Johnny, you gonna be okay?"

"It's practice Mom, what's there not to be okay about?"

"No, not practice, are you going to be okay with Olivia being gone?" I asked.

"Oh yeah, I mean not seeing her at my games cheering me on will stink, not having her to drive me around will stink also, but we have texting, so I can talk to her anytime I want. Plus we have the beach house and Disneyworld to look forward to for Christmas. Hey, how long is she off for Thanksgiving? Why aren't we seeing her then?"

"She is only off from Wednesday until Sunday, Dad's looking into an airline ticket, we may surprise her and bring her home that weekend if we can swing it. Otherwise she has already been invited to her dorm mate's house. She is from a little town very close to the university, so it's only a few minutes' drive for them."

"I hope we can bring her home, I'd hate for her to have a holiday dinner with someone else's family. You can take money from my savings Mom. Hey, are you still going to make a big fancy Christmas dinner when we go away? You never did tell me the plans you guys made for break." Johnny sounded concerned.

"First of all your money is for a car and college, I would never touch it, and you better keep adding to it when you can. Second of all, every time I wanted to share our plans you were too busy to listen. So now that I have your undivided attention, here are the plans." I said a little sarcastically.

"Last day of school before break is a Friday. We're leaving home around 5am on a Saturday and should be at Olivia's dorm by 4pm with hopefully only a couple stops for gas and bathroom breaks. We will have dinner near her school and then continue to drive straight through to Florida. I think it's another nine or ten hours from there so with all of us taking turns driving and napping and again, taking a couple stops for gas and breaks we should get to the hotel by early Sunday morning, we can check in and crash for a few hours if we need to, then we should be good to start checking out Disney. We have a pass to see three of the Disney parks. I figured we could do one each day then we are leaving sometime on Wednesday evening to head to the beach house which is only two hours from the hotel at Disney. We are staying there the whole week, so we will fill up the kitchen with groceries for all of our meals and still have a traditional Christmas dinner on Saturday. We will head home the following Wednesday and be home sometime Thursday so you still have four days before you go back to school Monday. Oh ya, and that Saturday after we get back, we are having another Christmas with family up here and we will do gifts then also instead of trying to bring them along."

"How will Olivia get her presents?"

"Oh, she is coming back with us and doesn't have to return to school until January 11th, that's why Dad is worried about the plane ticket in November because we need one for January"

"See then it won't be so bad waiting to see her when we have so much to look forward to, love you, Mom. See you later." He said as he climbed out of the truck.

As I drove home I couldn't make my mind stop wandering and I cried, hard. I drove right past the house so I could get myself together before I saw Derek and Dakota again. All I could think about was Olivia and my other kids. I wonder how much longer Kayla will live at home. I mean she is old enough to be on her own, she could decide to move out with one of her friends any day now, and then how often would I get to see her? Derek and I have joked about when the kids get older and move out what we will do to each of their bedrooms, but it always seemed so far off.

Actually we had told the kids that we wanted them to pay for their own college and they could live at home rent free as long as they were going to school. We meant the community college across town, then possibly doing their other two years at another college that is only forty five minutes from our house, there are several in the Cleveland area to choose from.

Well, Kayla never liked school and chose to work at the airport, originally she checked bags and tickets then they offered her the flight attendant school and she is so happy with her decision. It's not far from home, so it works out for her to still be with us. Olivia talked about being a nurse practitioner. I was a little nervous about what she would get into with student loans, but we wanted the kids to earn their own way so they would work hard and appreciate it more. I knew her grades were awesome, but had no idea that she would get an entire scholarship to pay for her schooling. The only problem with the scholarship is that it took her to a school out of state. Actually four states away! I guess I just never thought that far. I figured the kids would go to school close to home so they could live with us and save on dorms or rent and food plans. I figured they'd graduate and finds jobs close to home so we could have Sunday dinners together, go on camping trips together all summer, and just always stay a close family. This was my first reality check to a plan I've had for a very long time. And it was gonna take some getting used to. I drove around the block, wiped the tears from my saddened face, and headed back home. When

I got there I went in the house and searched for Bo's leash.

"Come on boy, let's go for a real walk." I went into the yard and kissed Derek goodbye. "We are going over to the park, it's time I got Bo used to his leash." I explained. "I'll be back in time to pick up Johnny."

"Okay, Honey, I think that's a good idea. After you finish did you want to just grab a pizza and a movie for tonight and relax?" He asked.

"That sounds great to me, Honey. I love you."

"Sounds good, Babe, Forever and always." He replied with a big grin.

"Forever and always." I repeated back to him with a forced smile.

Bo and I arrived at the park at 4pm. It was another beautiful afternoon for a walk. I figured we could walk for about two hours, then pick up a pizza in town on the corner at that pizzeria where they always have a pepperoni pizza ready to go. We will then get Johnny by 6:30 on our way back and eat by 7pm.

"Oh yeah and we'll rent a good movie also." I said out loud to the Bo as if he could understand me.

Chapter 6

As we pulled into the parking lot of the park, Bo immediately saw people walking their dog and started to get excited. I often feel so terrible that I have a ten year old dog that still isn't behaved on a leash or around new people. We have just always been able to take him in our own woods for exercise so he didn't need any restraints. This is the main reason why when we go camping he stays with my parents because if we took him with us we would be limited to what we could do at the campgrounds. We see other people with their dogs right in their canoes with them or swimming alongside, but Bo hates water. Funny because he is a lab, but Bo is different than other dogs. I parked and got the leash on

Bo, and then we jumped out onto the stone lot. I leaned back into the truck and grabbed my water bottle from the cup holder. As we started to walk you could see that Bo definitely didn't like walking on his leash too much. And I think he was especially bothered by the stone lot so we headed onto the paved walkway. He pulled and looked at me then would look at the woods to our sides almost pleading for me to give him some freedom to run and explore.

"Come on boy, you really have to get used to this or I may have to send you to doggie boot camp!"

He continued to drag me and I continued to tighten on his choker as a warning to slow down and walk with me

"Heel!" I called to him and he would walk by my side for all of five seconds then begin to pull forward again.

I continued to pull on his collar and tried to keep him walking smoothly. He was ok except for when he saw other dogs and people, then he pulled and whimpered and tried to drag me to them.

My mind went back to Olivia again. I knew I would be sad when Olivia left, but this was ridiculous. I couldn't stop myself from worrying about her. I had this sickening empty feeling in my gut. Was her flight going to be ok? Would her ride pick her up at the airport and get her to the dorm safely? Would she like her new roommates? Or more importantly would they like her? I could drive myself insane with all the thoughts that went through my head. She was going to call me once she got to the dorm but with her flight and one layover in Charlotte it was gonna be awhile before I heard from her.

"Stop it, Bo, heel!" Nothing worked and I wasn't in the mood to fight him.

I looked around and noticed a walking path leading into an opening to the woods. We headed off of the paved walkway because the rangers watched closely to be sure dogs keep their leashes on at all times on the open paths. We then followed one of the more secluded trails into the woods. Once we got a little ways into the woods, I removed his leash. He was so much happier without the leash. I just figured I would work with him more on another day. Today, I was missing my little girl. Thoughts were going through my head about her and the other kids growing up.

What a great time we always had together and how much we all liked to laugh. I could remember their first steps, first words, first days of kindergarten, every holiday gathering, it was all so clear and had all passed by way too quickly. I walked through the beautiful wooded park and continued to think back on wonderful memories with my family. One particular memory stood out and I couldn't help but smile as I started reminiscing in my mind.

I just love having parties at our house. Once Derek's oldest brother, Brian, and his family came home from Alaska for Thanksgiving. We really wanted to make it memorable since his kids hardly ever got to see all of us in Ohio. We decided to do our Christmas gift exchange also since we usually mail the kids presents and don't get to see the looks on their faces when they open them.

Then we decided to take it another step farther! Since it was also my niece's birthday three days after Thanksgiving, we decided to celebrate that too! Derek, the kids and I decorated our dining room for Thanksgiving, our family room like Christmas with a small Christmas tree to put the gifts under for the gift exchange, and then in the living room we hung streamers, balloons and "Happy Birthday" signs for the birthday girl and we even baked and decorated a cake for her!

As family arrived they were very pleased and in awe with our work. We moved from room to room throughout the evening celebrating each holiday in its perspective room. We started by having our Thanksgiving dinner in the dining room. It was such a great meal if I do say so myself. The turkey was good and moist, and so was the stuffing, boy do I hate dry stuffing. Olivia made the mashed potatoes and there were no lumps in that or in Derek's gravy. Derek loves making the gravy; he feels that's the manly part of the meal! Kayla experimented on a couple new recipes for a wonderful cranberry casserole and sweet potato casserole that everyone must have agreed was good because the dishes were licked clean!

After dinner we all helped clean the kitchen then we moved into the family room for "Christmas". The kids handed out all the gifts for the gift exchange and we took turns opening our gifts and sharing with the rest of the family. My niece was very anxious to move to the living room for her birthday party and cake, so we didn't waste any more time and moved there next. She was simply delighted as she opened each gift. Then we sang "Happy Birthday" and cut the cake. It was so good. It was a fantastic evening, we even joked that we should have worn our Halloween costumes and added one more holiday that we don't always get to share together! We had such a great time!

Bo and I had been walking for what seemed like forever and I decided I should head back the other way before it got too late when suddenly, I noticed Bo was gone!

"Bo!" I yelled for him. I whistled.

Nothing. I was so busy daydreaming I had lost him. And worse than that I realized I was no longer on the trail. And I had no idea how long I had been off of it.

"Oh my God, I can't believe I let myself do this again! Bo!" I yelled out loud.

Then another whistle. He always came when I called, especially when I whistled. I tried to stay calm, but this was unfamiliar territory for both of us. I didn't have my husband's blue dots to follow, I had no real idea even how long I was walking, and my dog was missing!

"This really sucks!" I said out loud. I tried to figure out by where the sun was at what direction I was going. I looked up, the woods were pretty dense, but I kind of guessed which way was west, and headed where I thought the truck might be.

I came to a deep ravine that I either had to climb down the steep hillside and then up again if I wanted to keep going the same way or I had to change my direction. This was definitely not the way I came to be here.

"Bo!" Where was that dog? He never left my side this long. Suddenly, I heard a rustling in the trees, and I saw his black coat hopping through like nothing had happened,

"Where were you?" I looked around trying to figure out which way we should go.

I figured my truck was west of where I was because I know when I parked the sun was behind me and when we first walked away I walked in the front of the truck. But then when we decided to go off the pavement and onto the wooded trails then which way did I turn?

Man, I was so confused. I walked along the edge of the ravine deciding if I should attempt it or go back the other way when suddenly my foot caught some soft dirt and I started to slide down the steep embankment.

"Bo!" I yelled.

I tried to grab tree roots as I slid, but they just slid from my hands. I was going so fast I couldn't snatch anything in my grasp. Next, I felt my legs crash into something, then it seemed to suck up most of my body and I came to a sudden stop.

I couldn't move. I turned to look and saw that I was trapped under a tree that had fallen on the hill and I had slid under it up to my waist. I was jammed in pretty good. I couldn't move at all and when I tried there was excruciating pain. My shirt had rolled up and my stomach was burning from the dirt and branches I slid over. I looked around. Bo had slid down the hill also. I think on purpose though, and was by my side.

I was face down and I could see blood all over my arms where I had slid over debris the whole way down the hillside. My legs were burning so they too were probably pretty cut up. The worst pain I felt came when I tried to free myself. It wasn't from the actual weight of the tree being on me, I could breathe fine, but I was pinned tight between the tree and the ground and the pressure hurt my back. It was just across my torso at my waist, my arms were up above my head and I could kick my feet so I don't think anything is broken, but there was no way I could get out from under this tree.

I tried to wiggle to slide out, not only was there no room, but the pain was intolerable. I must have hurt my back pretty bad. How could something like this happen? I didn't even think I was walking that close to the edge. Probably these stupid worn tennis shoes! Could I actually lay here and die because the pain I feel could be my insides all smooshed up? Crazy thoughts raced through my head. I needed to calm myself down. I was so uncomfortable. I was able to tilt from one side to the other just enough to gently pull my shirt back down over my stomach so it wasn't exposed to the bare ground. Then I heard it. My phone started ringing in my pocket.

"Oh my God, it's Johnny!" I said out loud as I heard his special ring tone. Crap, I was so freaked out about being lost I forgot I had my phone to call for help and now I couldn't get to it! I can't believe I was walking that long and didn't know it, how deep did I get into the woods?

I bet it was close to 7pm, and Johnny was wondering why I wasn't picking him up from practice. His coaches were going to get on him about not being picked up on time, and he would have no idea why I couldn't be there, and why I wouldn't be answering my phone! It rang three more times.

"Call your Dad's phone, Johnny." I thought intensely.

They will both then realize something has happened to me and come looking because I am never late for anything, especially my family.

I was feeling really thirsty. I tried to lay still and collect saliva in my mouth to swallow all at once to get rid of the cotton mouth I had. Bo didn't move. He just lay by me. I wish he were like Lassie in the movies, I could send him for help, but he would have no idea where to go for help. We both had to wait.

I started thinking of different things to do to get unpinned from under the tree. I had no wiggle room at all.

"These things only happen in the movies." I said out loud.

I looked all around me, and I suddenly saw something I had forgotten about. It was my water bottle. I must have let go of it while I was falling. It was fortunately only about six or so inches away from me. I grabbed a thin branch that was lying near me and stretched it out and swooshed it around the bottle and dragged it toward me. I took a small drink, then quickly closed it not knowing how long I was gonna be stuck here. What was I thinking? I can't be here for a while I need to figure out how to get out of this mess, no one will think to come looking for me down this ravine!

"Well, Bo," I said, "I wish I would have taught you how to dig on command so you could dig me out of here."

He got up and came closer toward me wagging his tail like we were gonna play.

"Oh I wish we could play boy, we will soon."

He flopped down so close to me he was almost on me and I ran my hand over his soft black coat.

"Your fur is always so soft, Buddy…" Then came the next ring tone, "Forever and For Always" by Shania Twain. It was my Derek. I started crying, there was no way to answer, no way to let him know how badly I needed him. I tried as hard as I could to move, I just couldn't. What would he be thinking? Would he know to come looking for me? He knows I came to the park. He knows I always answer my phone. This was killing me! I just needed to hear his voice! Johnny must have called him when I didn't answer and now he is also looking for me. Then the song stopped. And that was it.

"Oh Bo, what am I going to do, I could die out here and no one knows where we are!"

After that I felt very dizzy, my head started throbbing and the light hurt my eyes. I must have passed out because I was suddenly in my kitchen with Olivia, Kayla and my Mom making our big Thanksgiving dinner.

"Stuff the turkey right before it goes in the oven, Olivia," My Mom told her. "We don't want to take any chances and give any bacteria a chance to grow."

"Oh Mom, we have always been ok, it will be fine." I calmed her.

"Well, all the people that were talking on the news this morning were giving all these great hints and I just want this to be a nice dinner for Papa." She began to cry.

My Dad had just been diagnosed with lung cancer. The doctors weren't sure how bad it was. They were doing surgery next week to remove a small portion of his lung, and hopefully see that it had not spread anywhere else. My mom feared the worst because he had been coughing a lot for a while and he said it was nothing and refused to go to the doctor. Then, finally, when he started to bring up some blood she convinced him to go and the news was shocking. He never smoked a day in his life. Now she wanted him to have a nice family dinner. I'm guessing because it may be the last. We made sure to have all his favorites added to the meal, of course, Thanksgiving was his favorite meal of the year so it was an easy request to fill.

"Everything is gonna be just fine Mom, you'll see.

"Grandma, nothing gets Papa down, he'll kick this for sure!" Kayla said as she peeled the potatoes.

"I know girls. Your Papa is gonna beat this just like when he got through the war and came back to me so we could be married." She looked at her beautiful diamond wedding ring and produced a halfhearted smile. Derek leaned in the kitchen door,

"Don't forget to save me some drippings from the turkey ladies so I can make my famous gravy!"

I threw my kitchen towel at him, "Okay honey, we'll call you in about five hours when the turkey is done, now go play."

All the boys were out riding the four wheelers in the woods.

"Why don't you girls go out and enjoy the afternoon." I said to Kayla and Olivia as I slid the turkey in the oven, "We really shouldn't do much more until the turkey is closer to being done."

"That's okay Mom, we would rather stay and help you and Grandma bake Papa's favorite pies." Kayla insisted.

My sister, Nicole, who is married to Derek's brother Evan and their three boys arrived next. They live right up the street from us and we have always been very close. The boys all went outside and Nicole stayed inside and helped us. We hung out together all afternoon in the kitchen and talked and baked pies. We made one apple, one pumpkin and one cherry. Dad's traditional favorites.

I am so happy with the double oven Derek bought for me. It's so easy to cook different foods at the same time, and so much easier to plan meals. I love to bake together with my family. I used to have to make some of the things ahead of time, now we can do it together while the turkey is in the other oven. Derek's sisters and their families started showing up each bringing with them a side dish or another dessert. He has three sisters, Amy, Colette, and Faye. All three sisters and their families live very close, the farthest one is Colette and still she is only fifteen minutes away. Derek's Mom brought wonderful homemade rolls that she always makes from scratch. With a family as big as ours we always accept offers for everyone to bring something! We sent most of the kids outside and all of the men.

All of us girls hung out with a glass of wine, ice water with lemon for the girls, visited, set the tables, and finished making a fantastic dinner. Then we called everyone in and arranged everyone at the tables by their place cards that my niece had made and the origami turkey looking napkins some of the kids tried to fold together. My father said the blessing just like always...

"Dear Lord, bless this wonderful dinner made by the lovely ladies of this family. And also the gravy made by Derek. It's Thanksgiving Day and we can see the rewards of love and togetherness you've bestowed on our family. Let us all be aware that all our gifts come from you, and may we serve your heavenly will in all we do. Please stand by us during this time as you have always done in the past. Thank you for giving me such beautiful daughters and also for bringing into our lives the Logan family who has brought my girls two wonderful husbands who together brought me my precious grandchildren. And Lord, most of all thank you for helping me find my soul mate who has stuck with me for just over a half of a century

and hopefully for many more years to come, she has been my greatest gift for without her none of us would be together on this day, Amen."

When I opened my eyes, it was pitch black all around me. I actually awoke to my phone ringing again. Derek. He must be worried.

"Oh Honey, please come looking for me if you aren't already, I need you more than ever." I cried out loud in the dark.

Why was I having memories of my Dad? Was he with me? The cancer was worse than we had thought and took him three weeks after that last meal we all had together. It hasn't quite been a year since we lost him and my mother hasn't been able to move forward. They were together fifty six years and married for fifty two of them. We had just started getting her interested in joining the senior center in our community. Our first appointment is on Tuesday for bingo, I need to get out of here so I can go with her and help her meet new people.

I tried to think what I was going to do. Nothing. There was nothing I could do but wait for someone to come along. But would they? I left the path, this is all my fault. I am so stupid. My thoughts got the best of me and I was careless and now look what's happened.

My phone rang again. Olivia. I told her to call when she got settled in her dorm. Well, at least I know she's alright. Oh man, she will try Derek when I don't answer and then she will know what's happened and she will be worried her first day of school and I didn't want her to feel obligated to come home.

Her song from me is "My Wish" by Rascal Flatts. I gave her that one for her graduation. It says something about roads leading you to where you want to go, and when faced with choices, to take the one that is most important to you. But my favorite part mentions that if a door closes in front of you to just find a window. I hope no doors close and keep my kids from their dreams. I wonder where my window is right now?

"Oh, what a mess I have caused. I have such a terrible headache. I just want to go home."

Chapter 7

    I must have fallen asleep because when I awoke the sun was up. I had no idea what time it was. My headache was gone though and that was good. It was quiet in the woods except for the birds singing. I could scream, but I doubt anyone would hear me so I didn't want to waste my breath or get any thirstier.

    "Bo, can you get help?" Again I wished animals could talk.

    He just stared at me with his big brown eyes. I know he understands and he is probably thinking that he is lost also so how can he help me? How could I be so dumb to leave the trail? I was so busy thinking all my crazy, sad thoughts.

Happy thoughts, I need to think of happy times, I am tired of being sad.

"You know, Bo, everyone loves our house. That's why we love to have parties there. Everyone has a good time, and you are such a good dog!" I started to cry again. I didn't care anymore and I screamed at the top of my lungs,

"Please help me!"

Bo got up and ran away.

"Come back, boy, please don't leave me alone, you don't know where you are going!" I continued to cry.

My stomach was starting to rumble. All it knew was it was time for breakfast, but I didn't even care. This is weird for me because I love to eat, usually like every three hours. I just wanted out of these woods and I wanted to be home.

I couldn't see Bo anymore. I hope somehow he knew what he was doing. I was so scared, and so weak. I looked around as much as I could to see if maybe I could hear anyone on the trail. Maybe it was closer than what I originally thought. Maybe no one has just come for a walk yet, and as soon as they do, I will hear them and then I will scream and they will look over the hill and see me, then they will get help and I will be okay and get to go home to my family.

My phone just kept ringing, one after another. I almost wished that the kids didn't put those special ringtones on it. I was keeping count in the dirt in front of me how many times someone called by the different rings coming in. The problem was there were so many, and I felt so awful and sad that I couldn't just answer the darn thing!

Derek called the most. I missed him so bad. I know he can do anything, he could help me if he just knew what happened to me, but he doesn't. My heart broke more and more as my husband and kids kept calling me. My mother, my best friend, even my dentist! Yep, Olivia put a special ringtone in for everyone. I am sure that was just an appointment reminder. I tried to laugh, but just couldn't, this was not a joke!

I hope they were out looking and not just calling. I wish I could just get my phone out of my pocket and tell them all where to find me. Then a strange feeling came over me and I felt like I was somewhere else. If I was sleeping again I didn't want to wake up, but it didn't feel like sleep and I hoped I wasn't dead. But for some reason I felt at peace and didn't care because I was back at Olivia's graduation. One of my proudest moments;

I looked around me and my whole family was there to watch her take valedictorian of her class. Olivia was her senior class president. School always came so easy for her. She was liked by everyone. As she delivered her speech, which I had listened to many times while she practiced, she had changed her ending to something I had not heard until now.

"...and in closing I mostly want to thank the two most influential people in my life. Mom, Dad," she looked right at us, "You guys have been my rock. Without all of your support since the very day I was born I would have never had the courage and strength to achieve all I have. I can only hope to be as good of a parent to my own children as the two of you have been to my siblings and me. I love you both...Forever and Always."

My phone, it's ringing, it's our song it's him again, I tried so hard to wiggle, I needed to get to that phone.

"Damn it!" I yelled. "I hate this!" It stopped ringing. I was in a lot of pain. I must have passed out.

I am hungry and thirsty. I better take another small sip of my water it's been awhile and I am probably getting dehydrated. I was thinking if I could maybe dig a trench around my waist with the stick I grabbed my water bottle with, but it was too flimsy, maybe my fingers were strong enough. If I could make myself loose enough then I could possibly be able to get out from under this mess.

I tried to dig my finger nails into the ground around me. Not only has it been a nice hot summer, but I was also happy that it hadn't rained a lot to ruin our camping trips. Now I was wishing it would have because the ground was so hard I wasn't able to dig away any of the dirt.

I was lying so flat to the ground; it was actually too painful to move my arms all the way back to my waist where the tree was pinning me down. I really wasn't sure how long the tree was because I couldn't even see the trunk or the top of it as far as I could turn my head to either side. To my right I could see the branches and the leaves. Not too many, it looked like it was probably dead like the ones in our woods. To my left the tree was covered by brush so who knew where it ended.

I was thinking about stupid things just to have something to think about. For instance, how many ants did it take to build those little mounds of dirt they live in? They sure are hard little workers. I wonder if they have brains? They must have them to be able to work together so well to build such amazing tunnels and mounds. When I was a kid I loved wrecking their little mounds and watch them scurry all over the place. I would always wonder what they were thinking, like

"Run, run it's a giant!" Or "Oh here we go again everyone gather the dirt and rebuild!"

I tried to manage some sort of laugh at myself, something I did pretty often. I actually thought I was funny, some other people did also, especially Derek. I could always make him laugh with the stupid things I did and said just to see his smile. The funniest part about me was I could usually crack myself up even when I was completely alone.

I sometimes wondered what people were thinking if they drove by me and saw me laugh when no one else was in the car with me. I just love to laugh and be silly. It's not letting go of the kid inside. I definitely didn't want to act my age unless I had to. Like now.

Right now I needed to act my age and try to think of a plan to get out of this situation. I continued to try to excavate the ground around my waist with my fingers with no luck at all.

It just seemed useless and I felt so defeated. I folded my arms under my head and made a pillow. I felt like I should be kicking, screaming for help, trying to dig more, anything to free myself. But I just laid still. There was nothing I could do but lay quiet and hope to hear someone on the trail, and hope the trails are closer than I want to think they are. I can only imagine what's going on back at the house. I just know my family is worried and could only imagine the conversation they'd be having right now. It would go something like this…

"Did Mom answer her phone yet?" Johnny would ask his Dad.

"No, I went to the park and found the truck, but I couldn't find them. I yelled, I whistled. I didn't even hear a bark from Bo. I know she is out there. I have a feeling she is lost or even hurt in the woods somewhere, but the rangers and the police won't start looking for 24 hours, they say she could have left the truck and went with someone else willingly.

These people don't know your mother, she would never leave us." Derek would be holding back his tears. He did this well when he was upset. He was a very caring person and truly loved all of us, so when emotional things happened I could catch him sometimes out of the corner of my eye fighting a tear or two.

"I knew something was wrong when no one was there to pick me up after practice." Johnny would add. "Mom is never late and would never just forget any of us."

"Everything will be fine, boys, we need to keep our heads straight." Derek would reply.

"So are they gonna start searching around dinner? That would be 24 hours." Dakota would ask.

"Yeah" Derek would tell them both. "But I'm not waiting, I'm going back now, come on guys, and make sure you have your cell phones. Let's go find Mom."

At least I hope that's how it would go, and then they would come find me! My phone was ringing again.

"I'm here, please find me." I said out loud.

It was Kayla. Her song was "It's my life" by Bon Jovi. She came up with that because she didn't ever want to go to college. She never liked any part of going to school and always begged me to home school her. I refused, of course, because I felt she should be there to socialize, but she hated it. Kayla has always liked to do her own thing. She is very happy with becoming a flight attendant and doesn't mind going to classes because she loves everything about it. Knowing this career will allow her to see the world. How exciting is that?

When I was young, I used to want to work on a cruise ship. I thought it would be so much fun to meet all the people and see all the ports. But because all I ever really wanted was to be a wife and mom, and I was good with numbers, I decided to go to college and become an accountant so I could settle in one place after school and hopefully meet someone to share my dreams with. And then I met Derek. That's when I knew all my dreams would come true. My sister, our best friend Beth and I were in Myrtle Beach on spring break, it was my senior year of college. We ran out of suntan lotion and ran to the local Wal Mart. He was in the aisle reading the suntan lotion bottles…

"Is it true that an SPF of anything over 30 doesn't work any better anyway?" He asked.

"I think I heard that once." I replied barely able to look at him because he was so hot!

"Well, I don't like smelling like I have sunscreen on, and this one has an SPF of 45, but it's a sport so it's supposed to be sweat proof." He continued to talk to me like we knew each other.

"Sounds like that one is the winner, I however, love smelling like a coconut so I will get this one." I laughed, and so did Beth and Nicole.

"Are you guys from around here?" He asked.

"No, we are from Ohio."

"No way, so am I, where about?"

"We are near Cleveland." I could look at him now. Wow did he have nice eyes!

"Same here, I live in a town called Andover. Ever hear of it?"

"Hear of it, I grew up camping at Pymatuning Lake State Park.

"That's wild, so did we, my Dad told my mom it was crazy that we always camped ten minutes from home, but she loved that

lake, she said it was better than Lake Erie because it was gentle, but you could still enjoy being by the water." He went on. "We would go there from spring until fall, almost every weekend because we lived in a small house on a small lot of land and my Mom wanted us to have a place to run lose and still be safe and within a distance we could hear her whistle for us."

"We were there a lot during the summer, but we also went to different places too, like Sandusky, Pennsylvania, and the best was canoeing on the Mohican River, and having our camper right on the riverbank. I always have loved camping."

"So what city are you from?" He asked with interest.

"It's called Mentor. We are right by the Lake Erie so I know what your mom means when she says the water gets rough."

"I can't believe we live so close, yet we run into each other in South Carolina! Would it be pushing it to get your number so I can maybe contact you when we get back home?"

"Okay!" I hope I didn't sound too excited. I can't believe I gave my phone number to a stranger I just met in another state. But something felt right. Like I already knew him. I was willing to take a chance on

him. "I am graduating from Ohio University next month and then I will be back home in Mentor. I will have a degree in accounting and I will be looking for a job close to home."

"That's great. I am actually graduating next month from Penn State with a business degree. I am going to join my dad in his construction business, maybe we could use and accountant." He winked.

"Come on Abby!" I heard my sister yell down the aisle.

"I better go, it was nice to see you, I mean MEET you." I said blushing.

"It was good to SEE you too, I'll call you when I get back home after graduation in May." He smiled. What a great smile!

The day after graduation I wondered if I would ever hear from him. And then he started calling. Several times. We talked on the phone every day for about a month. Then one beautiful, sunny day in late June my sister and I met him and one of his brothers at the State Park we all used to camp at.

We parked up front by the office and went for a walk by all the camping sites.

"Man, I love this place, I want to get a camper and bring my own family here when I have one." Derek said.

"Me too." said Nicole.

"Yeah me too, it hasn't seemed to change too much since I was here last." Evan added.

"When was the last time you guys came here?" I asked them.

"Let's see, I think I was eighteen, once I left for college I would come home in the summer and work so much I never felt like coming up to the campground, Evan here, and I did construction with my Dad and we wouldn't get done till dark almost every night so we just showered and crashed during the week, so then on weekends we just slept in then did all the yard work to help out my Dad so he and Mom and my little sister could still enjoy the whole weekend here. We didn't miss camping anymore and it was nice to have the house to ourselves when everyone else came up here to campground. So I guess it's been four years, it doesn't seem like that long, man time flies when you're having fun as they say. I haven't even been here to walk. You take for granted when something is so close to you, you forget about how beautiful it is and how many great memories it added to your childhood. What about you two? When were you gals here last?"

"Oh we were just here last summer. My Mom always books site fifty-nine right next to

the beach. She said when we were little she liked that spot because she could see us at the beach and the playground without leaving the campsite and she could still see my Dad fishing on the pier This will be the same spot I reserve also." I said as we walked over by site fifty-nine, then over by the beach, and up along the play area.

"Here's where we used to have this awesome game of volleyball every time we were here. Remember that Evan?" Derek announced at the volleyball court.

"Oh yeah" he jumped and pretended to spike an imaginary ball over the net. My sister giggled and blushed.

"We did too!" I was wondering if he played with me as a kid. "There were two kids in my family, just Nicole and me and four boys in my aunt's family. We always came together and played this family that had a lot of kids. There were three boys and three girls all in the same family. They were all close in age. And their names were some sort of puzzle or something so their mom remembered them, what was that Nicole? It was so much fun!"

"It was like the order of the alphabet or something funny like that I think." She answered me but was staring at Evan still as

he was goofing around on the playground like a kid.

Derek was looking at me in disbelief. "Please tell me you didn't wear pink wrist bands so you wouldn't hurt your wrists when hitting the ball?"

I couldn't believe it! "No way! I mean Yeah, I always did! You are not those kids?"

"Um, yeah, I think we are. There is Amy, Brian, Collette, me, then Evan, and Faye and we are all almost exactly one year apart between our ages, and we played volleyball every summer, right here, with two girls and four boys!"

"Oh my God! That's crazy." said Nicole.

"I had the biggest crush on you but I was always afraid to talk to you." Derek revealed.

"Which one were you?" I asked. "I barely remember what anyone looked like back then." I said.

"I always wore my sleeves cut off my Nike t-shirts, and Nike tennis shoes. And I had my hair spiked up, and blond tips."

"Oh my God," I laughed. That was you? You always tried to act so tough, but you were so skinny my mom wanted to bring you back to our camper and feed you extra

s'mores to fatten you up." We all laughed. "Man did you fill out!"

"Thanks" he chuckled "My Dad said I didn't get my height until I was 18 and then I just sprouted up. I had always played football and there was so much working out, with a lot of running, I was eating everything I could get my hands on and it seemed like I burned right through it, then after my senior year of football was over all I did was lift weights, not a lot of cardio. My height jumped five inches and everything I ate just all turned into muscle, here hit this."

He lifted his shirt for me to hit his six pack. Man was he ripped! Yep, he sure did grow up. Evan lifted his shirt also, and I thought Nicole might faint because I think he took her breath away for a moment. These were two really hot boys, even if they were just showing off!

We hung out all afternoon, and continued to double date....

I felt something wet all over my face. It was Bo licking my face.

"You came back!" I was so happy to see someone, even if it was just a dog.

He was my dog, my best friend. "Did you try to get help Boy?" I asked as I noticed his paws and legs were soaking wet.

Good he found water. I was debating about sharing what little I had. I love my dog, but I needed to realize I had to worry about myself so my kids and husband wouldn't be alone if I could prevent it, but I cared for him so much I would feel evil not sharing.

He laid down next to me, and put his head on my arms. I wonder where he had been? Was it a stream or lake he had found? I guess it didn't matter to me in my current situation. It seemed like we laid there in the quiet for hours. I wanted to talk but I was getting too thirsty and didn't want to waste all of my water to quick. Bo would look at me out of the corner of his eye, then straight forward, then sideways again. I smiled at him and he picked up his head and licked my face.

"Ewe, Bo yuk, you're slobbering all over me." I said with a laugh and patted him on his head. "I love you, Bo. You are such a good dog. If you were smart you'd leave instead of staying here with me". I just couldn't stop thinking about Derek and the kids. I wonder what they were doing now. I closed my eyes and forced more of my

memories to cover up my
pain…Pymatuning…

*Derek and I were camping at
Pymatuning one warm summer evening
exactly two years from our first date there.
We had decided to spend that same weekend
there for as long as we were together since
that was the place of our first date. Even
though the sun rose on Pymatuning Lake and
there was no sunset it was still always
beautiful in the evening. Derek and I were
coming back to our tent from our evening
walk around the campground. Derek sat in
one of our lawn chairs by the fire pit.*

*"Come here, Abby, there's something I
need to show you." I went to him and sat in
the chair beside him. He had a duffle bag
under his chair I hadn't noticed before. He
pulled the bag out from under his chair and
slowly unzipped the zipper.*

*"What's up with you, Honey?" I asked
quizzingly.*

*"Do you know that each color of a rose
means something?"*

"What do you mean?"

*He reached into the bag and pulled out
a small zipper sandwich bag full of white rose*

petals. He sprinkled them across my lap and said,

"The white rose petals stand for innocence, purity and new beginnings. This explains our relationship." I smiled and shook my head as he continued to pull out each bag one by one and he sprinkled each bag of petals on me as he explained the meaning of its color...

"Orange is for desire and I definitely desire you, Yellow is for warmth and happiness, I always want to keep you warm and happy, Pink is for grace and elegance, this one describes you. And finally, Red, the rose color that means love and romance."

He knelt down on one knee, and I covered my opened mouth cause I knew what was coming. He pulled a long stem, dark red rose from the bag with something shiny hanging from it,

"I love you Abby, and I would love for you to be beside me through life, will you marry me and be with me forever and always?"

My eyes teared up, I blinked a few times so I could look into his beautiful eyes and said "Of course! I love you Derek, I will love you forever and always, this is so awesome!"

The ring was absolutely beautiful. We started the plans immediately. We were both so excited we planned to get married the following June, our regular weekend at the lake. We wanted everything to be there. Our place.

"And, I want a picture of our wedding party in front of the lake, just like it is tonight." I said as I pointed to the lake that was so calm it looked like glass...

I felt movement across my arm and it woke me up again. It was Bo, he was moving slowly and cautiously as he came to his feet. He walked around me. Then he held still and just stared into the trees. His tail stood sharp so I knew something was wrong because he always wagged it.

"What is it boy, you hear something?" I whispered timidly.

He started a low steady growl. I didn't know if it was someone or *something* that he was hearing. Then I heard it also. A rustle over in the bushes. I didn't know what to do, yell for help or stay quiet. I better yell, hopefully it's human.

"HELP!" I yelled with all my strength. "Over here, help me, I'm stuck!"

Then it appeared, and it wasn't human at all. It was a coyote, and he didn't seem any happier to see us than we did him. He was showing all of his teeth and looking back and forth between Bo and me.

"Get out of here!" I yelled trying to scare it away.

I felt so helpless. Bo started to bark and went right after him.

"Bo, don't! Come back!" I didn't know what to do. That stupid animal is either gonna get to me or my dog. And if he gets to the dog, then he will definitely get to me.

The coyote must have been startled because he turned around and ran back into the woods, and Bo kept after him.

"Oh God, please bring my dog back safe." I was hoping there weren't more waiting in the woods and that was just a decoy to get the dog away from me. I was shaking so hard it hurt my body, I could barely catch my breath I was so nervous and scared.

There was something I hadn't tried yet. Praying to God for help. I probably don't have very much pull since I haven't been in church since the spring. I go all winter faithfully every Sunday. I used to even help teach the preschool kids Sunday school before church and I'd sing in the choir. Then when spring hits, we get so busy with camping, and yard work, we just don't go every Sunday.

With Derek being so busy on the weeknights we cherish our weekend time, and although church is only an hour and a half, if you count the time getting everyone ready to go, getting there, then talking to the other members afterward, you can't just leave as soon as it's over cause that would be just plain rude. It actually takes up four hours of your Sunday morning. Now we just go once in a while to keep up with things and to feel connected. We also volunteer at all the events our church provides for the community like pancake breakfasts and chili suppers, and help fill the food pantry for needy families. I know I have too many excuses for not going. I need to make time for God. I will make that more of a priority if I get out of this mess.

I remember one perfect day in church. It was the day Derek and I got married. Nicole and Evan were engaged soon after we were and we decided we all wanted a double wedding in a church with the reception to take place at the lake. Nicole and I wore big white flowing bridal gowns and our grooms were in white tuxedoes. We had ten people in our combined bridal party comprised of Derek and Evan's brother Brian and four of their best friends as ushers, and then their three sisters and two of Nicole and my best friends as bridesmaids. The girls wore pink colored puffy dresses and the men wore grey tuxedoes with pink cummerbunds and bowties. Everything was puffy in the eighties, especially our hair!

We were lucky to have the most amazing weather. After completing the ceremony at the church the Logan's all grew up in out in Andover, we all went outside to take pictures then went to Pymatuning beach for the reception.

The caterer had raised a large white tent complete with lights, round tables and chairs, and a dance floor. It was decorated beautifully by my mother and new mother in law and we had two cakes. Our cake was white with pink roses and green leaves. It had four double layer cakes that were separated with pillars between two sets of cakes and a fountain with lights and pink water flowing underneath. It was three different flavors. The largest bottom cake and the top one that we would keep and eat on our first anniversary was basic white wedding cake, which seemed to be most popular at that time. The next largest tier was carrot cake with walnuts and cream cheese filled center, and the last one was a lemon cake with lemon crème center.

Nicole and Evan loved chocolate, so their cake was four layers stacked just like ours but all different chocolate flavors. The bottom tier to serve and top for saving was basic chocolate cake, with a fudge center, the next tier was German chocolate with a coconut filling, and the third tier was devil's food cake with a cherry filling. Both cakes were on the same table and had a set of plastic stairs from each going to one center two layer cake. Yep, one layer chocolate and one was white. This was our "unity" cake. To us this was uniting our families together, forever and always.

This was Nicole and my idea instead of having a dessert table. Once the cake was cut the guests had many flavors to choose from and we didn't have to worry about extra desserts. The cakes looked so decadent together on the table. We also had a savory dinner of strip steaks or grilled chicken, red skin garlic and butter potatoes, fancy green beans and salad with rolls. We even had a live band for dancing into the evening. It was the most beautiful day and I have to admit I have never seen more amazing pictures. Even with all our puff! And I also got my group picture on the lake I wanted, and the lake was calm like glass again just like when Derek proposed. It was a perfect day.

Enough daydreaming already! There are so many thoughts going through my head you'd think I had someone to talk to. My phone made a funny noise. What was that?

Oh no, I realized right then exactly what that sound was, the battery was going dead. I heard that some newer phones had tracking devices on them, but I wasn't sure if mine did, if it did they would have found me by now though so it must not. I needed to think of something. Oh yeah, I should say a prayer, man I get my mind on other things too easy out here…

"Dear God, I know it's been awhile, but as you can see I am in a little bit of a tough situation and I really need your help." I began. "Please help my family or anyone at this point find me. I really don't want to die here all alone. I have so much to look forward to in my life. I have a wonderful husband and four great kids. I need to be home so I can continue to help Derek with our family. My family needs their Mom back, and I need them, badly."

I started to cry, but there were hardly any tears, I was becoming too dehydrated. But I pulled myself together and continued,

"Give me the strength I need to pull through this. Please help me with the challenges I need to face, and please guide someone to find me. Also help my Bo get away safely from that animal and bring him back to me. Amen."

Man I wish my Dad was here. He is a much better prayer than me.

Where was that dog? The good thing was I hadn't heard any more growling and I never heard any yelping, so hopefully he was just chasing him far away and he'd be back again. At this point my hunger had faded. It felt like I had been here for a week, but I only remember one night of darkness, unless I slept right through one. I was so tired and so weak I don't know how many times I have dozed off, and I don't know how long I have slept when I do. I closed my eyes and more memories flooded my head.

It was just over a year ago. We were celebrating our 20 year anniversary camping

at Pymatuning for the weekend as we had continued to do every year as planned. Although by this stage in our lives we had upgraded camping gear several times through the years from a tent, to a pop up camper, to a 26 foot Dutchman and currently our beautiful 31ft Cougar. The kids informed us that their gift to us this year was a dinner and dance cruise on a four level cruise ship in Cleveland on the Cuyahoga River and on Lake Erie. It's called the Goodtime III. We had gone on the two hour daytime cruises through the years but never the four hour dinner and dance evening cruise. We had always wanted to try one but never got around to it, so this was a much appreciated gift!

The following weekend when we arrived to the port, there was no one around.

"Are you sure it sails tonight?" I asked Kayla.

"Oh yeah." She replied. "I think we are just running late, come on hurry up."

We hurried onto the boat, and Kayla and the kids directed us through the first floor and up to the dining level. When we got to the top of the steps everyone yelled,

"Surprise!"

"Oh wow, what's all this?" Derek asked.

"This is great!" I added. "Who did all this?"

"Happy Anniversary, we hope you like it. We reserved the entire ship for all of us! We will have dinner and dancing and they take us through the river and out on the lake for four hours!" Olivia said excitedly.

"I love it!" I shouted with a smile. Our parents, siblings and their families and it seemed all of our friends and neighbors were on the ship with us! Everything was decorated like a wedding reception, it was all so beautiful!

The captain showed us to our table. It was all decorated just like on our wedding day. As we got over to our table there was another table on the side with a beautiful cake stacked five cakes high and frosted with fondant and flowers cascading from the top to the bottom like a spiral stair case in all shades of pink. It was so beautiful, almost too beautiful to eat.

"Abby" Derek said. "Look at that cake!"

I love cake, especially wedding cake. I always wished I was talented enough to decorate them and be able to attend all kinds of weddings and be able to set them up, then cut them and serve them to all the guests. It's just a weird fantasy of mine I guess.

"Who made that?" I asked.

"I think the captain baked it himself." Johnny joked and we all laughed.

"This was such a great idea." I said excitedly.

"Well, this reception is for you and Derek only." said Nicole with a smile. "If you wouldn't have needed that sunscreen on spring break I would have never met my soul mate and had my wonderful kids!"

"I'd share my day with the two of you again anytime!" I smiled and hugged her really tight. Evan shook Derek's hand and then pulled him in for a hug.

We ate an incredible dinner buffet. They served chicken piccata, sliced roast beef and gravy, garlic red skin potatoes, green beans, salad, and of course an assortment of rolls. At each table there was a box of chocolates that said:

Abigail and Derek Logan
June 24, 1989 - June 24, 2009
"Forever and Always"

After dinner we walked around the outside of the ship and saw the lights of

Cleveland at night. I remember it all so well. The Rock and Roll Hall of Fame, the Browns Stadium, the Science Center and other tall amazing buildings. What gorgeous lights. You could barely tell you were on the boat while inside, but outside you could feel the warm summer breeze in your hair and against your face and hear the waves break against the sides of the boat.

"What a beautiful night." I commented. "Oh Derek look at the lighthouse." I absolutely love lighthouses. I always tell Derek I would like to go visit each and every one of them. My Mother-in-law came out to the deck.

"I think they are playing your song so you two can start the dancing" She said as she floated her arm toward the door.

"That's funny, Derek, it's our song from our 1989 wedding, Glory of Love!"

"So, Abby, let's not waste this music, are you ready to dance?"

"Sure Honey, Mom grab Dad and let's show these kids how it's done." I said as we all worked our way to the dance floor.

Right after that song was played, the DJ played our latest favorite song, Forever and For Always, by Shania Twain. We stayed on the floor and held each other tight. I have loved Derek more with every year that has passed, and just when I think I can't possibly love him anymore than I already do, I look at him, he smiles and I do! Forever and always, that's for sure. We danced to all of our favorite songs. Slow dances, fast dances, line dances. It was such a good party. I love watching people have a great time. I don't think anyone stayed in their seats, including my kids. They all love to dance.

When it was time to cut the cake, Derek and I walked over behind the cake and everyone gathered around. We cut the cake and fed it to each other with our arms intertwined, and then he gave me a big kiss, and dipped me back. Everyone clapped and cheered and there were even a few that whistled. He loved showing how much he loved me in front of people, and I loved it when he acted like that.

"Mom, the cake tastes great, don't you think?" asked Kayla.

"Oh yeah, although I don't think there is a cake I don't like." Everyone began to hit their forks on their glasses, like at a wedding when they want you to kiss each other, so Derek leaned over and gave me another big kiss, just as I shoved a big bite of cake in my

mouth and everyone clapped again. He is so funny.

"So are you two having a good time?" My mom asked.

"This is so great," I answered," Thank you so much."

"Don't thank us, your kids planned everything." She said. "Even the boys helped. They have been working on this event for almost a year. All we did was help Derek's parents pay the bill. Kayla made the cake, isn't it great? You two have really raised some great kids!"

"They sure are, Mom! And, Oh my gosh Kayla, really? When did you learn to do this?" I said excitedly.

"I have been taking classes to do wedding cakes mom, just like you always wanted to do, but you were too busy. When you talked about it, I just realized I would love to try something like that too and wanted to surprise you. I figured I could make cakes for weddings and you can help me transport them and set them up so you can be at a lot of weddings like you always said you wanted!" She gave me a big hug. "I love you so much, Mom."

"This is all just so awesome! You kids are all so talented." I held back tears so my make-up wouldn't run.

My great kids. What were they doing right now? I am so tired I hope someone finds me soon.

Chapter 8

Again I started to think what everyone could be doing back home. Were they out looking for me? Had it been long enough for them to call a search party? Every time my phone had rung and I didn't answer, did they wonder what happened to me? I always answer my phone, and if I can't I call back as soon as I can. And now my phone was dead.

I tried to figure out how long I had been laying here. I just can't. I thought about that first day. When I realized I was off the path. Why didn't I call for help then? But I didn't realize I was in any danger. I figured I couldn't be too far off of the path, and then I fell down this stupid hill. I felt like I was sliding forever. Then to end up stuck under this tree! What are the chances of that happening? I am very lucky though I guess. I mean I could have broken something and I could have a bone protruding out of my skin and have bled to death. What a nice thought. Yuk. I have always been very lucky in my life. I know Derek will find me soon. I started to close my eyes and force more memories so I did not have to be with reality at the moment. Derek doing anything and everything.

He always mastered anything he tried. When we would ask how he could do things so well, without ever doing it before, his answer was always the same. He would say

"I know the theory behind it, if you know the theory, you can do anything."

I would always just shake my head and smile. I don't know if I was jealous because I wasn't as good as he was, or if I was just so proud that someone that talented was mine.

Once he went on a golf outing with the guys from work. He had never played real golf, just miniature golf with me and the kids. Anyway, he beat everyone, and the guys he was with were seasoned players. He had told me that evening how they all picked on him and said he lied about never playing. He replied by telling them that the reason he was so good was because he had no handicaps and was just there to have fun. He looked at the ball, saw where it needed to go and hit it. Things were just that easy for him.

If I asked for anything he could build, he would build it. I have ideas in my head, but I can't put them to paper. Derek has a way that if I describe it, he draws it. Then after asking me if that's what I meant, which it always is, he makes me sign the drawing before he does the work. He thinks he's funny. He really makes me so happy. And he even helped me have four wonderful kids. The boys have his talents. I can see them gaining more every moment they spend with him…

"What's that?" I opened my eyes abruptly to more rustling in the bushes.

Maybe Bo had come back. No, it's like all the bushes and trees are moving.

"Oh no, there is a storm coming!" The trees were starting to bend in the wind around me. I could tell it was getting dark, but it was only the middle of the day because I had just caught a glimpse of the sun before the clouds covered it up. I was getting worried about more of the old, dead trees falling.

"Not like two trees could fall in the same spot." I tried to make myself feel better.

Of course that could happen. Anything could happen. I just wanted to make myself believe that it couldn't. I could hear thunder getting louder and started to see bright lightning flicker. How does that go? If you count the seconds between thunder and the lightning it will tell you how many miles the storm is away from you? Or is it how many minutes before the storm reaches you?

Actually, who am I fooling, it's not like I can go take cover or anything! Oh this is not going to be fun. The storm rolled in as the trees twisted and bent, and their leaves were falling all around me. The rain came down pretty hard for quite some time. I was able to turn my head enough to get my mouth good and wet and got a good drink. It was worth all the scary noise to feel my mouth moist again and not worry about running out of what little water I had left in my bottle.

Although it didn't seem too hot it had been somewhat uncomfortable, even being covered with the trees around me, I didn't realize how much the heat and humidly had been getting to me until I felt the cool water drizzle over me.

"Oh, keep it coming, this feels so good!" The rain stuck around for what felt like hours, and when it stopped the sun reappeared and it was cooler.

That would be a nice break. I decided to try to dig around my waist again. It still wasn't soft enough for me to dig out around me with my fingers. I wonder if I could use a thicker branch it would be stronger than my nails. Now if I could only reach one. The twig I used to pull my water bottle over to me that first day already proved to be way to flimsy so that was a lost cause and there were no other ones even close. So again, I just laid there and took in what was around me.

It's amazing how you can hear so many noises that you don't pay attention to when you're just walking the trails. I have seen so many different species of birds. There have been blue jays, cardinals, sparrows, robins, mourning doves, and other birds I don't even know, just beautiful. I hear them all day long, but I don't know whose song belongs to whom. If I make it out of here, I will study birds and songs. I also hear frogs. At least I think its frogs. I wonder if am close to water? Maybe the same water Bo found. Where is he? I hope someone found him and he's okay. The butterflies. I have seen monarch butterflies the most, I heard once they love to be around milkweed so it must be close by.

"Oh my God I am rambling to myself in my head like a crazy person! Is this gonna drive me truly insane?"

The one thing I do want to hear, a person's voice, isn't there. I would do anything now to hear anyone's voice. I would love to hear Derek's voice, or even the kids bickering a little. I just feel so alone.

Chapter 9

I opened my eyes, and it was too dark to see anything. Night time. I am still not sure how many nights I have been here. I am going to think this is only the second night. The time has been so slow. I am not one to lie around. I am always on the go. I wish there was some way of knowing what Derek and the kids were doing, I am sure they are looking for me. The truck is in the parking lot to the park. But this is a very large park, I was so out of it thinking about my little girl growing up and going to college, I just wasn't paying any attention how long I was walking. My Olivia. She is so pretty and smart. My first child to go to college. Kayla hated school, Olivia loved it.

Amazing how different your children can be after you raise them exactly the same. Kayla was working hard at the airport, she was always better with a hands-on way of learning. That is why this flight attendant program is perfect for her. And she loves it; it's all she talks about when she gets home.

And the cake decorating, it makes so much sense for her. Kayla got her first job when she was only fourteen. She always liked to make her own money. She washed dishes at a small town restaurant. She is a better worker than me. I would hate doing dishes all day, especially other peoples, and smell like a greasy spoon! I never thought she would stay there long, but she did that job for two years and during the summer she also worked the local drive in during the evenings. I actually think working at the drive in all summer kept her out of trouble because she never had time to get involved in parties with working every night until one or two in the morning. She had saved enough money to buy her own first car when she turned sixteen, and loaned money to Olivia to buy her first car when she turned sixteen.

Olivia worked at the Yellow Submarine, a sub shop in our town. She didn't have as much saved up as Kayla, but was able to make payments to her of $100 a month for twenty months and had her little Honda paid off before she left for school.

Now she won't need it for a while since you can't have a car your freshman year, but she will need it on breaks, and for next year.

Breaks. Oh no! They have to find me. We have such a great trip planned for Olivia's first break. I wanted to do something really fun, that we had never done before. Most of our family vacations were camping trips. We all loved camping so much. But this one was different. This was one of our biggest trips ever. I wanted to make sure the kids would all be able to go and all would be old enough to remember it.

Derek and I actually never had a plan to go to Disney. No desire to see Mickey and his friends. I laughed to myself. But Olivia and Johnny always wanted to go to Florida and Dakota and Kayla love all the amusement park stuff, so this just seemed to be like the perfect trip. We were all going to leave from home and drive to North Carolina and pick up Olivia and possibly spend a little time there by her college so she could show us around or just keep driving if we aren't too tired. Dakota is also thinking of going there so he would like to see the campus. He is also thinking of

Penn State like his Dad. I am secretly hoping for that one so he will be closer to home, but I will let him make the final choice. After we check everything out there we will continue to drive to Orlando.

We have a three day pass so we can see each park and we are staying at the nicest resort they have with all of our meals included. Now that's a vacation for me. With camping, Derek and I still have to cook a lot and I have to plan all the meals. Next, we are moving over to the coast to a beach house. We are all so excited! It's all we have talked about for months. Knowing the girls they will be so helpful with the cooking and cleaning there and if there is a grill then all my men like to cook outside so I will definitely pick up stuff for them to make…

"Oh my God, someone has to find me soon! I won't miss that trip!" I yelled out loud. I felt a little hungry again, but tried to think of other thoughts to make the pains go away. I just closed my eyes, and laid my head on my crossed arms.

"Mom, this one looks beautiful." Kayla said about one of the beach houses we were looking at online.

"Yes it does, now let's see how many bedrooms, oh here it is. There are four bedrooms. That should work out okay, right? Who would share? You and Olivia or the boys?"

"Olivia and I can share, right Liv? Kayla asked.

"Yeah, we can share. Do any of the bedrooms have an ocean view?"

"Yeah, actually two of the bedrooms take up the entire upstairs with windows on one side overlooking the ocean. The other two are road side on the main floor. I don't think the boys are too worried about an ocean view, they would probably rather have the first floor rooms anyway because they are next to the rec room with a pool table, video games, foosball, and a ping pong table and if they stay downstairs I could care less if they stay up all night cause I won't hear them. Plus as long as we are there and they have food they will be happy!" We all laughed.

"Wow that place is neat! It is so close to the water. Look at the availability calendar and check it for our break. I can't wait!" Olivia remarked.

"Yep, it says it's available. Ok, then this is the one. Let me make a phone call to get some more info. Olivia can you do a map *for us from Orlando to this house to put in our trip packet I am making?"*

"Sure, Mom. But we could just put the addresses into the GPS."

"We'll use that also, but I don't always trust it, so if we have all our maps together if anything goes array we will have a backup plan." I reminded her also about the campground and cornfield story.

She giggled and went to make me a map. One time is all it takes for something to go wrong for me and from that moment on I will be sure to have a backup plan or try a new way. I always joke with Derek that I wanted to go on a trip with only an atlas like when we were first married. There was no internet or GPS, or cell phones to help you find your way. You found it all yourself with a road map. Our kids probably couldn't even read one.

Mental note... bring along road map for trip and try to find everything with that first. We will save the GPS and internet directions as our back up plan. I want my kids to be well rounded and understand more of their other options incase technology fails them.

I must have dreaming, because when I opened my eyes it was light again, but very chilly. The evenings and early mornings were just starting to be colder and seemed to stay dark longer. My guess would be about 7:30 am, although I truly had no idea. I glanced to my other side, and to my relief, there lay Bo. I was so happy he had returned safe. I wonder if he was finding any food for himself. Maybe he ate the coyote, I smiled to myself. I wanted to call his name and wake him, but I would wait for him to wake up on his own, not like we had somewhere to go.

I turned my head to the other side again and listened hard, hoping to hear someone calling my name, but of course I didn't. I tried to use my fingers to dig around my waist again now that we had a good rain. The ground wasn't much better.

Then there was another sound I hadn't heard yet. It was up above me, I struggled to turn so I could look through the thick trees, up toward the sky. And there it was, up in the air. It was a helicopter! They are looking for me! This is great! But a helicopter will never see me. The trees make too much cover. At least that means people are looking though. I hope they come soon. Now this is bitter sweet. There is no way I can get their attention from down here. I hope they have some sort of special seeing device that they can look right through the brush and see me.

But I doubt it. Bitter sweet. Funny saying isn't it? I never used to understand what the heck it meant. I guess it means it *could* be sweet, but something else is thrown in to mess it up and make it also bitter. So yep, that's exactly what this helicopter is. It is sweet because they are looking for me, but bitter because they probably can't see me. I still feel better though. I am just hoping that the helicopter is there for me and not just out on a joy ride, or whatever helicopters do when they aren't trying to find a missing person!

The *swooshes* of the giant propellers woke up Bo. He got up and walked around me, and licked my face.

"Oh Bo! I am so glad you came back!" I said with delight. "Now I have someone to talk to instead of myself!" I had an idea.

"Hey Bo, go get me stick!" His tail began to wag and he ran off sniffling around in the bushes.

He came back with a nice, thick stick, about two feet long.

"Perfect! Bring it here boy." I said. He came closer, then about a foot from my reach he stopped and stared at me.

"Bo, come on boy, give me the stick." He just stood there and wagged his tail like I could lunge for it as I always do.

"Come on Buddy, bring me the stick!" He dropped it on the ground! Crap, I knew I should have gotten a trainer to get him to learn to bring the stick all the way to me! I was hoping I could use the thicker stick he got to dig better around my waist and help loosen the soil and maybe pull myself out.

"Bo, get the stick Boy," He ran off again.

Now where was he going? He ran into the weeds and rustled around a little, then emerged with another stick. I started to cry, but my cry turned into a laugh. Not a funny laugh, but one of those *I'm gonna die here and rot so I better make the best of it* laughs. I just wish he understood what I needed him to do. He could probably even dig me out with his paws if he knew I needed him too. But that silly old dog just piled up sticks just out of my reach each time I tried to get him to bring me one closer.

I needed a new plan. I came to the realization that maybe I would never get out of this mess. Soon after something even more terrible happened. I felt my chest getting tight, and I began to wheeze. Oh no, my asthma was kicking in. With the humid and moist weather, not much to drink, the weight of the tree pushing against my chest, and no medicine for a couple days, my symptoms were kicking in.

"Oh my God," I said out loud, "Please don't let me die out here!" I tried to take slow steady breaths.

Chapter 10

"Dad, come on," Dakota yelled. "I see our truck. This is where she went in."

"Let's go!" Derek waved to all the searchers. "Down this path."

Everyone ran down the path through the woods looking and yelling.

"Abby!" They yelled one after another. But no answers were heard.

"Bo, come on boy, where are you?" Derek yelled more.

"Mom!" Kayla was crying out. "Where could she be, what happened to them, why aren't they here?"

There must have been over 100 people searching. Some were on the path, some off.

All looking under bushes, around trees. But finding nothing.

"Dad, we need to get more people involved. Maybe the news." Johnny said.

"I've called everyone, guys, we'll find her. Dakota, come with me this way, Kayla and Johnny go that way. Yell for Bo and Mom, hopefully one will come or answer."

As Derek moved through the woods yelling and looking he suddenly saw something.

"Dakota, look there!" *It was a black, hairy mound."*

"Dad, no, it can't be." *They ran over hoping it wasn't what they feared, but it was. It was Bo. He was dead. Derek checked him out.*

"It looks like nothing got to him, he must have just died from hunger or dehydration. I'm not sure."

"Dad, look!" *Dakota screamed.* "Over there under that tree!"

Derek ran over and grabbed me by the head, "Nooooo! *He screamed out loud looking up to God, why did you take her from us?"*

****

I woke up shaking uncontrollably.

"Oh my God! I was just dreaming!" I was still having trouble breathing. Now my heart was racing as well. "I refuse to die out here Bo." I whispered to him as he lay by my side. "And you better not die either. Come on boy, let's breathe together."

I calmed my breathing and my heart by slow breathing in through my nose and out through my mouth. I ran my hand over Bo, feeling how soft his fur still was and hoping he had found water while he was away from me. I still wanted to share mine with him just in case, but there wasn't a lot left and to try to share I would probably dump too much out. I felt so selfish. I had to give him some. I tried to pour a little on the ground and it sucked right into the still dry dirt.

"Here boy." He came close and when I went to pour some in his mouth he pulled away. He must know I need it and won't take it. Or maybe he knew where he found some before and still goes to it when I sleep. I hope so.

"We are gonna make it, boy," I said. I looked around at my surroundings. Not like I hadn't done this before, but now with more intense thoughts of getting out of my situation. There was just nothing for me to do but wait. What are the chances of this happening to anyone? I kept thinking of how I fell and still can't believe the only thing keeping me here is this stupid tree that I can't move!

At least I hope my back just hurts from the fall and it's not broken somewhere. That would be terrible with all the things Derek , the kids and I like to do. I would go crazy if I couldn't remain active. Am I supposed to die this way? Is this how my wonderful life was supposed to end? To starve to death, or to have an asthma attack take my breath away? I could feel myself getting worked up again, so I calmed myself down and started to take the deep slow breaths again. It worked well if I just stayed calm. That was something that was definitely getting harder to do as the time passed. I again tried to wiggle out.

"Heck, if I am here a few more days I will lose some more weight and I will be able to get right out from under here." I laughed softly to myself and Bo just trying to be positive about anything I could, but it wasn't making me feel the least bit better. I really was so tired.

But then it happened. I did feel myself move. It was just a little, but I did, I moved. It was happening. I probably really was losing weight and was able to shift a little.

I twisted to the left about an eighth of an inch, then to my right. Oh but the pain was excruciating. I must have broken something. As I moved there was intense pain shooting up my back. "Okay, maybe not such a good idea. I lay still with my head on my arms. Man, I hope they find us soon.

One our favorite places to camp was on the Mohican River. We went to the same place each summer. About six years ago we met two other families and now we meet them back there every year. We all have kids in the same age range and thought it would be fun to meet up once a year at the same spot. Our families all meshed together very well.

Our family always got there Tuesday night and the other two families meet us on Wednesday afternoon and then we all stayed until Monday of the following week. We have enough canoes, kayaks and tubes for us all to go down the river together. We would make it an all day trip. Along the way we would take breaks at different camping sites that had little snack shops set up along the river banks and visit with other people that we met along the river. We were always very excited to make this trip. Especially Dakota. He had started to like one of the girls from one of the other families. Her name was Alicia. She was very beautiful and super nice so you couldn't blame him. They kept in touch throughout the rest of the year by emails and texting on their cell phones. Now that he has his license I wonder how long before he would want to make the drive to see her. Mohican was two hours from our home, but Alicia lived right in between us and the campground, so that was only an hour. Dakota wanted to invite her to his high school homecoming this year, so Derek and I talked to her parents and we thought they could all come up and just bring their camper and stay in our backyard so we wouldn't have to worry about the kids driving so far back and forth the day of the dance and also that way they would be here for all the pictures and stuff. Back to camping...

Our first night in Mohican this past summer our family was alone as always. It was just after dark, so we built a camp fire. "Anyone want a s'more?" Olivia asked.

"I'll have two!" Johnny replied.

"Me, too!" answered Dakota. "But I'll have mine with a peanut butter cup instead of chocolate, Mom did you bring the Reese's cups?

"Yep, I'll go get all the stuff out of the camper, does anyone know where Kayla went?"

"She's on a bike ride with Dad." Olivia said. "Can I help you, Mom?"

"Just grab the s'more stuff and I'll get the fillings out for hobo pies, I am sure that's what Dad wants."

"Hey Mom, did you happen to get ice cream?" Johnny asked.

"Yep, it's in the freezer; let's get that out after we cook our desserts so it doesn't melt."

"Cool," he answered happily.

As we all sat down around the fire, Derek and Kayla returned.

"Hobo pies, my favorite, did you get peach pie filling, Honey?" Derek asked as he wrapped his arms around me for big hug.

"Oh yeah, and cherry." I said as I kissed him on the cheek.

"Mom, can you tell me how to make the pie with cherry and chocolate the way you like it?" Kayla asked.

"All you do is put some chocolate squares on the pie filling before the top bread slice, don't forget to spray the cookers."

I loved camping with my family. And they all loved it also. We went camping about eight times a year.

"So how are you guys liking the new camper Mom and I bought?" Derek asked the kids.

"It's so big, we have so much more space." Olivia replied.

"I love the bigger seating area. It will be better when it rains and we get stuck inside because we won't be sitting on each other." Kayla laughed.

"I love it Honey!" I had said. "It's like a home away from home."

It's not like we are ever in our camper, just to sleep and play games if it rains. But Kayla was right, there were some trips where it rained a lot, and you hate to go home so we would all cram into our old camper and pretty much sit on top of each other to play a game or watch a movie. This one was going to be much nicer. This year it only rained for a few hours during one trip, but it was great to have all that space when it did.

We sat around the campfire eating our dessert and played the game, "I am going to California, and I am taking a......" after saying that phase you take turns saying what you will take starting with the first letter of the alphabet, then as it advances to each person they have to say the phrase, say what the last person was bringing, then what they will bring that starts with the next letter of the alphabet. If you miss anything you are out. We have played this game since the kids were little, and let me tell you they don't miss any!

Dakota started, "I'm going to California and I am taking Alicia!" We all laughed. The game went on into the night until Derek and I could barely keep our eyes open. Derek and I went inside.

"Don't stay up too late guys, everyone will be here early tomorrow and we are planning on being on the river all day."

Just then I opened my eyes and caught a view of something in the distance. It was a deer. A very large deer. His antlers were towering over his head. He must not see me or Bo because he kept getting closer. Then behind him I could see several smaller deer.

"Aw, a whole family." Then just as quick as I saw them, Bo did also and he barked and jumped up and ran after them, growling with all his hair sticking up on his back in full "Bo style" attack dog mode. Oh that dog, gotta love him. I hope he doesn't scare off any potential rescuers like that!

Deer are so beautiful but very quiet. I am so glad that no one in my family hunts. I know that it is a sport and we especially need to get rid of some of the deer population, but it's so sad to see any life taken away. We should find a way to capture them and spay or neuter them so they just don't have so many running around. I am surprised those are the first ones I have seen. I guess I am glad I am not a hunter because if that's how long it takes to see a deer, I would get too bored with it anyhow!

My stomach was rumbling again, I was getting used to being hungry. I was so busy remembering good times that I actually forgot about my asthma and it wasn't bothering me at all anymore. Maybe it was more of a panic attack instead. I guess I have just realized there is nothing I can do about my situation and have finally become a little more relaxed. Actually for the first time since I knew Olivia was going to be leaving to go to college out of state, I felt some sort of peace coming over me.

Chapter 11

"Did you get him, Bo?" He looked very tired when he returned. "Hey at least you get to run around."

The sun wasn't as warm as it had been today. I could see it was right on top of me,

"Must be around noon possibly," I thought out loud. Then I heard another helicopter above me. "At least they are looking in the right area, Bo, we need people down here, not up there, there are too many trees for them to see us through. I wish I had some way of making them notice me."

"Bo, it looks like I am not going to get out of here. Maybe you should just run away from me and go find a nice family to take care of you."

I started to cry and Bo came close to me, and plopped down almost on my head. He leaned into me so close and just laid there, like he was trying to cuddle with me. Maybe he understood more than I thought he did. I really loved my dog. He just looked at you like he wanted to talk so badly. But all you needed to see was his eyes. And he would lean into you like he was hugging you. He is so loving. But then as soon as he laid into me, he jumped up and ran back into the woods again. I had gotten used to this.

By my guess, I have laid here for almost three days. I have maybe one small sip of water left in my bottle, so things aren't looking too good in the dehydration department. I have tried to wiggle free every time I have had the energy but with no avail. Now the energy is also gone. I know I can't give up or my time is done. I just don't know what else to do. Where is my Derek? He would know what to do. He always knows what to do. He has saved me so many times when I am in a bind with a project. He just always fixes everything for everyone. I am feeling so tired, and so weak…

"Derek!" I yelled.
"What, Honey?" He came over to me.

"I tried pushing the button to let out the slide and it stopped working."

We were on one of our last camping trips of the season with our brand new camper and suddenly the switch for one of the slide outs had just gone dead. If this slide isn't out all the way we can't get to the pantry that has most of our food in it, but worse than that because it started to go out before it fell into place to make a good seal we were worried that if it were to rain, and we were expecting some that weekend, we could have water in the new camper and have even worse issues.

Although we had camped for years, Derek was no camper mechanic, but I knew he would figure something out. Derek headed out to assess our situation. He grabbed his tools and crawled under the slide. As he did his thing I organized the kids to do their regular jobs. Kayla laid out our rugs that cover the dirt outside, Olivia and Dakota set up our canopy that we put over the picnic table and set the chairs up around the fire pit and Johnny unloaded the wood and kayaks out of the back of the truck.

I took out all the camper books and began to look up information about the slides. I hoped we could figure it out and it didn't put a damper on our last weekend. The kids were back in school so we were only staying till Sunday not Monday like we do in the summer months. We planned this trip because there was a hot air balloon fair in the town we were camping in.

"Honey, try the switch!" Derek called up from under the camper.

"Nothing." I said as I pushed on the switch.

"Okay, hang on." He replied.

Olivia came inside the camper and waited on the couch for our next directions.

"Mom, what if he can't fix it?" She asked.

"Well, I'm not really sure yet" I told her.

"What about food?" She inquired. Olivia liked to eat although you wouldn't know it with her size two frame.

"Well, we can get to the fridge so we can have eggs and toast in the morning. Then we can still have burgers before the fair for lunch, because I hadn't put the bread in the pantry yet. Then we will eat dinner at the fair, and Sunday morning we will just have more eggs." I said trying to be optimistic.

"But what about our s'mores and hobo pies?" She sounded almost nervous, she was so funny.

"Those are in the pantry." I said.

"Dad, do you need any help?" She called out with passion.

"You guys in there?" He asked.

"Yes!" We yelled though the window.

"Okay, one of you get on each side and apply pressure." As we did this the slide began to move out until we got it in the position.

"It's working!" We laughed.

When the slide was completely out Derek came over to the door and explained how he just disconnected the motor so we could do it manually. And we would have to get it fixed when we got back home. But now our trip will be the same as normal. He saved the day yet again. Some people may not think that's a big deal, but to me, it meant everything. That's how he was. He may not always know how to fix everything, but he could always make it work to get us by until we could get it fixed properly if he couldn't.

And if he was here now he would find a way to get me out.

Bo came running back from the woods barking at me, then ran back in like when we go for walks. He was just barking and wagging his tail like crazy as he went in for a few minutes then came back to me.

"What is it, Boy?" I asked. "Or *who* is it?" I got a little excited. "What are you barking at boy?" He barked and growled and was looking up the hill into the woods.

There wasn't a lot of underbrush which is how I lost my way off of the path. I could only see up the ravine and not beyond that of course, and I didn't see anything for him to bark at, so I thought maybe he heard something I couldn't. I prayed it wasn't that darn coyote again. I was too weak to yell. I was hoping if there was anyone there, they would hear him and come.

By this time I'm sure Derek has a missing person report in the newspapers and on the news, so maybe there are hundreds of people out looking for me. At least I hope there are, I don't want to die out here. I want more memories with my family. I was so upset about Olivia going off to college. I couldn't think of anything else except my kids growing up and moving away from me.

But being out here I have realized that it doesn't matter if my family is growing up. We still have so many things to share. So many more memories to make together, so many things to look forward to. I have to watch my sons football games coming up in the fall, I have two more high school graduations, Kayla's graduation from her airline stewardess school, and possibly three college graduations, hopefully four weddings, and then grandkids! Oh my God, grandkids, and I can do all this all over again with them! I want to live, please give me strength to yell. I took all the last bit of energy I had and started to yell,

"Help, I'm over here! Who is it Bo?" He was growling and barking like crazy. But he wasn't running from my side now and usually he ran after everything. What was he protecting me from? Then I heard them. Voices! Human voices!

"Down here!" I gave it all I had to give.

And then I heard trampling on the leaves and branches. Someone was coming from behind me where I couldn't see.

"Oh my God. She is over here!" One man said to the other. Then they appeared right in front of me.

Bo stopped barking as soon as they leaned over to pet him. It was Mr. Smith and another man!

"Oh I am so happy to see you guys!" I said as I started to cry uncontrollably.

"You okay, Ma'am? I mean as okay as you can be?" He had a southern accent, and a long unkempt beard. This must be Mr. Smith's brother, Bob, that Derek mentioned form West Virginia.

"I'm just hungry, and thirsty, and my back hurts a lot, but I am ok, can you get this tree off of me?"

"Bill, how far does this tree go?" Bill, also with a long beard, just not quite as long as his brothers, walked to where I couldn't see him, then he came back.

"You sure are a lucky lady," He said. "This ravine is pretty deep and this tree is huge! We are gonna need more help. Bob you stay with her and the dog, I'll go get help."

"Okay, Bill. Hurry back."

"Wait, call my husband as soon as you can, his number is 412-555-8842."

"We have his number, Ma'am, but we have no cell phone. I'll get in touch as soon as I get out of the woods, I will be back with help as soon as I can."

"Thank you, Mr. Smith." I said with all the smile I had left to give. I felt so much relief.

"Here's some water for you." Bob gently touched his canteen to my lips. It was so good to wet my throat again with really cold water. What little was in my water bottle was warm had not ever been refreshing. Then he cupped his hand and poured some in it for Bo and gave him a drink.

"He sure is a good dog staying with you all this time. If he wouldn't have come after us we wouldn't have known to come way down here to look for you!"

"Bo brought you to me? He does understand I was in trouble! Yeah, he ran off a few times after a coyote and a deer, otherwise he has stayed by my side. I just thought he was chasing another animal again. How far off of the path am I anyhow?"

"About a mile, why did you go off of the path anyway? Don't you know that's not safe?"

"I was just walking and thinking and daydreaming and I didn't know how long I was walking until I realized the path wasn't there anymore. I was trying to trace my steps and yell for the dog, he must have chased something off and I didn't notice him leaving me, I was just very upset. Then as I was trying to find my way out I came to this ravine and just hit some soft dirt, and these dumb old shoes, and well you see the end result. Do you know how long I have been here?"

"Yeah, I guess from what I understand it's been three days."

"That was my guess, also. Hey why don't you or your brother carry a cell phone?"

"Nope, we don't believe in them, you have one?"

"Yeah," I kinda chuckled. "It's in my pocket. It went dead though."

"Things don't work so well with no where to plug 'um in, huh?" He was trying to be funny.

"Or when your hands can't get to your pockets." I added sarcastically throwing my arms up as much as I could move them, which wasn't much.

"What's that pile of sticks over there? Looks like someone was gonna make a fire? But you couldn't possibly reach that far?"

"Ah no" I replied again with a grin, "My dog has never learned to finish a fetch, I was hoping he would bring me one so I could try to dig myself out, but none of them ever made it this far." We both laughed. "How did you hear about me?"

"Derek called to let us know he wasn't comin over to do any work in the bathroom cause of what had happened to you. We joined the search right away and have been looking all over the whole park with over half of the townspeople. Your family sure loves you and that dog. They have been hanging signs all over town and the park. A lot of people think you just left your truck in the park and left your family for another man. You know like an affair or somethin' so they weren't out lookin'. But there are a lot that believed you would never leave your family and you were hurt or something and they did look. Thought maybe you were kidnapped by the same guy that kidnapped that young girl in town, but when they found them out on the highway trying to leave the state you weren't with them."

"They found the girl? Was she alright?" I asked with some fear.

"Ya, she alright, except for being really scared and shaken and all. But they spent a lot of time questioning the guy about you and searching his house, they didn't spend a lot of time checking the woods till after that. Then when they finally started around these parts the problem is this park is so big and has a lot of walking trails so I don't think anyone thought to go this far off of any of the trails to look for you. And you're especially hard to see down in here with this here tree camouflaging your body. They may have been right up there and never thought to look down in here, who knows? They even sent up helicopters." He continued,

"Bill and I are pretty good hunters, so we decided we would make good searchers too, so we had the police show us maps of all the ground they had already covered and we got the idea that maybe you got off the path and just started walking into the woods. We were actually looking for about four hours when we heard your dog barkin and then he came running toward us then back toward the hill and back at us again like for us to follow him. We had seen pictures of him so we knew he would bring us to you."

"How long do you think it will take your brother to get some help?"

"I'm not too sure. He has to get back to the right path, and then track back until he finds someone. Like I said we walked for a very long time so it could be awhile. But you will be alright now. It's almost over and you will be back with your family soon. It may take some time, Lady, but Bill is the best tracker I know, he will go as fast as he can."

"I just can't wait to see my family, get off this ground and eat a hamburger!" I chuckled softly.

"Hey, I do have something for you."

He reached into his pocket and got out a granola bar. I tucked a few of these in here this morning when we left to go out. I always get hungry out in the woods."

He gave me and Bo each a granola bar. I am sure he was as hungry as I was. He wolfed it down wagging his tail and looked at Bob for more.

"Sorry, guy, that's all I have for now, I am sure you will get a bigger reward when we all get outta here." He said as he patted Bo on his head. Bo laid down and put his head between his paws.

"Thanks, that tastes awesome! I love peanut butter and so does Bo."

"So what have you been doing all this time to keep from going crazy?" Bob asked.

"Well, I have been watching all the birds and bugs. And I have seen a few animals, but when they see me or Bo they either leave or Bo chases them away. And mostly I have been just searching my brain for good memories in my life. I close my eyes and play the whole memory over in my head. It's so quiet out here; I actually see it as though it is actually happening again at that very moment."

"You have had a good life I take it?" He asked with a grin.

"I couldn't ask for anything better, and I am sorry I keep saying this, but I can't wait to see my family. I am ready to make some new memories. I am ready to enjoy the future. You know, people always say 'life goes by so fast' and I always agreed and was sad about it, but now that I have been through this I can see there are so many more things to look forward to in my wonderful life, and I can't wait to get out of here and live every minute of it!"

"Yep, I understand that. Sounds like you have a great plan. Hey Lady, I know your husband's name, but I didn't get your name."

"Oh I am sorry, it's Abigail, but Abby for short and this is Bo." I turned to where he was laying and he wasn't there. "Bo? Now where did he go? Oh well, he must have saw something again, hopefully he won't be gone when they get ba…"

Chapter 12

My kids were all around me. They were dressed very nice and they were all smiling. I turned to look by my side and there was the love of my life. The man I met as a child, and ran into again at the right time in my life. We had joined our lives together and brought in these four beautiful and loving children.

We raised them with love and a firm sense of independence and boundaries and now they were gonna be able to take this knowledge and start their own lives. As I continued to look around the room I saw all my family and friends sitting in pews of a church. What were we doing? Am I at my funeral? Then I turned around to face the preacher. He was holding a baby in long white gown. He turned to me and Derek and smiled. Then Kayla and a tall handsome man moved in closer to the preacher with Olivia next to them.

"Do you accept the responsibility to be the godmother to this child and be sure she follows the ways of God throughout her life?" The preacher asked Olivia.

"I do." She replied.

Oh my, did Kayla have a baby? Did she get married? Why am I seeing this? Oh the baby is so beautiful! My granddaughter?"

I woke up to more voices and had a smile on my face that no one was gonna remove, and tears tried to weep from my eyes. Bill had returned, with a lot of other people, At that instant I heard his voice. It was Derek!

"Abigail!" He yelled as he ran over and dived onto the ground next to me. He wrapped his arms around me and hugged me so hard it hurt, but I wasn't gonna tell him that. "Oh my God, I thought we lost you forever!"

"Mom!" I think I heard every one of my kids' voices at the exact same time, even Olivia, and then they hovered all around me.

"Mom, you are never allowed to go on a walk alone again!" cried Kayla.

"We had helicopters up, Mom, they couldn't find you, we were all so scared we had lost you forever!" Olivia wept.

"Johnny and I had both of our football teams out looking! We were all over this stupid park!" Dakota was talking in a crackling voice holding back tears.

Johnny couldn't even talk, he just held my hand tight and bawled.

"I love you guys so much, thank you for not giving up on me!" I cried

"Never!" Derek exclaimed loudly and they all agreed, even the Smith brothers.

Some firemen moved over beside me and had everyone move out of their way while they started checking my vitals and checking me for wounds. I told them about my back and then about my legs and stomach that had scratched and burned from my slide, but I could never see how bad they were.

"If everyone could just back away so we can get her out of here." One said. I lay there while a paramedic continued to check me out.

"Ok Abby, we need to get this tree tied off so we can keep it off of you while we cut it out of the way. Just stay calm."

Easy for him to say. I just wanted to jump up and hold my family.

"Mom, is Bo still with you?" Johnny asked.

"He was a few minutes ago, then he disappeared again." I answered. "He saved me you guys, when he heard the Smith brothers he went and brought them to me!"

"We have to find him, we aren't leaving without him!" The kids said to the others as they started looking and yelling for their dog as the rescuers worked on getting me freed.

It actually took about two more hours to get me out and onto a stretcher. Then as they were getting ready to lift me up to carry me out of the ravine I heard Dakota yell.

"Bo! Come here, boy!" But Bo ran right past all of them and toward me with a stick in his mouth, and laid it next to me on the stretcher.

"You're a good dog, Bo. You don't need any training buddy, you are smart enough!" I patted him on his soft head and with that I knew everything else was going to be okay.

"Derek?" I tried to look for him but was strapped down to the stretcher.

"I'm right here, Abby." He was by my side.

"I love you." I said weeping.

"Forever and always" He replied and grabbed my hand.

"FOREVER AND ALWAYS!"

THE END

Or is it??